# Digital Scholarship in Education

This book is an essential guide to multimodal theses and dissertations (MTDs) which involve researchers working with digital data such as video. Brendan Jacobs explains how MTDs provide new methodological options which can improve both the visibility and quality of research, and then provides a how-to guide for anyone interested in writing an MTD or engaging with digital scholarship. It helps readers understand how digital scholarship can generate insights into learning and contains links to examples of best practice in digital scholarship.

Embracing the new methodological possibilities that a purely digital environment provides, this book sets a much-needed precedent for using multimodal approaches in your own research, from classroom practice right up to PhD level.

**Brendan Jacobs** is Head of Department – STEM Education, at the University of New England. His research interests include STEM education, explanatory animation creation, conceptual consolidation and digital scholarship. Brendan is currently conducting a longitudinal study integrating STEM education in primary schools (https://silo.edu.au/).

# Digital Scholarship in Education

Multimodality as a Window into Learning

**Brendan Jacobs**

LONDON AND NEW YORK

First published 2024
by Routledge
4 Park Square, Milton Park, Abingdon, Oxon OX14 4RN

and by Routledge
605 Third Avenue, New York, NY 10158

*Routledge is an imprint of the Taylor & Francis Group, an informa business*

© 2024 Brendan Jacobs

The right of Brendan Jacobs to be identified as author of this work has been asserted in accordance with sections 77 and 78 of the Copyright, Designs and Patents Act 1988.

All rights reserved. No part of this book may be reprinted or reproduced or utilised in any form or by any electronic, mechanical, or other means, now known or hereafter invented, including photocopying and recording, or in any information storage or retrieval system, without permission in writing from the publishers.

*Trademark notice*: Product or corporate names may be trademarks or registered trademarks, and are used only for identification and explanation without intent to infringe.

*British Library Cataloguing-in-Publication Data*
A catalogue record for this book is available from the British Library

ISBN: 978-1-032-58177-4 (hbk)
ISBN: 978-1-032-58264-1 (pbk)
ISBN: 978-1-003-44932-4 (ebk)

DOI: 10.4324/9781003449324

Typeset in Times New Roman
by SPi Technologies India Pvt Ltd (Straive)

# Contents

*Preface*   *viii*

**1 Multimodal theses and dissertations**   1

   *1.1 Introduction 1*
   *1.2 Constructionism 2*
   *1.3 The Storyboard project 3*
      *1.3.1 Research question 3*
      *1.3.2 Research methodology 4*
      *1.3.3 Methods – Explanatory case study 5*
      *1.3.4 Data analysis and results 7*
   *1.4 The affordances of online publication 8*
      *1.4.1 Access to all of the data 8*
      *1.4.2 Digital appendices 9*
      *1.4.3 Patterns in the data 9*
   *1.5 The Networked Digital Library of Theses and Dissertations 11*
   *1.6 The United States Electronics Thesis and Dissertation Association 11*
   *1.7 A transdisciplinary protocol for digital scholarship 12*
      *1.7.1 Location 13*
      *1.7.2 Maintenance 14*
      *1.7.3 Academic governance 14*
   *1.8 Theory in practice 15*
   *1.9 Conclusion and recommendations 17*
   *References 18*

vi  *Contents*

## 2 Provisional multimodal research   20

    2.1  *Introduction* 20
    2.2  *Multimodality* 21
    2.3  *The SILO project* 22
    2.4  *PMR methodology* 23
    2.5  *PMR methods* 24
        2.5.1  *Chronology of digital files* 25
        2.5.2  *Researcher's reflexive journal* 25
    2.6  *Referential chronology* 26
    2.7  *PMR data analysis* 27
    2.8  *The role of provisional data* 28
    2.9  *PMR practice* 29
    2.10  *Critiquing PMR* 31
        2.10.1  *Practitioner action research* 33
        2.10.2  *Design-Based Research (DBR)* 33
        2.10.3  *Autoethnography* 34
        2.10.4  *Arts-based research* 34
    2.11  *The design cycle* 35
    2.12  *Conclusion and recommendations* 37
    *References* 38

## 3 Guidelines for digital scholarship   41

    3.1  *Introduction* 41
    3.2  *Domain names and DOIs* 42
    3.3  *Web design* 44
        3.3.1  *The use of templates* 44
        3.3.2  *Cascading style sheets* 46
        3.3.3  *Static v dynamic websites* 47
    3.4  *File management* 48
        3.4.1  *Guidelines for file management* 48
        3.4.2  *File transfer protocol* 49
        3.4.3  *Leveraging your metadata* 49
    3.5  *Working with images* 50
        3.5.1  *HTML image maps* 50
    3.6  *Website structure and navigation* 51
    3.7  *Search Engine Optimisation* 53
    3.8  *Intellectual property* 54
    3.9  *Issues related to ethics* 55
    3.10  *Working with supervisors* 56

3.11 Exemplars 56
3.12 Constructive alignment 57
3.13 Conclusion and recommendations 59
References 60

**4 Digital pedagogy: The educational affordances of using digital devices**   62

4.1 Introduction 62
4.2 In search of a definition for digital pedagogy 63
4.3 The educational affordances of using digital devices 66
    4.3.1 Duplication 68
    4.3.2 Reversibility 69
    4.3.3 Iteration 69
    4.3.4 Collaboration 70
    4.3.5 Representation 70
    4.3.6 Dissemination 71
    4.3.7 Virtuality 71
    4.3.8 Searchability 72
4.4 Digital pedagogy as part of a pedagogical toolkit 73
4.5 Multimodality as a window into learning 74
4.6 Conclusion and recommendations 77
References 78

Index   82

# Preface

Digital scholarship marks a move away from printed materials so a book on the subject might seem to be a contradiction in terms. Ultimately, this is a question of terminology but also an exploration of practice. It has been ten years since former US President Barack Obama created a directive to make publicly funded research freely available (Holdren, 2013). Since that time over 4.5 million digitised theses and dissertations have become accessible online. Searching online for a "digital thesis" can provide access to millions of digitised theses which have been saved in a digital format such as PDF. It would be hard to imagine that a researcher in this day and age would conduct or report on research without using digital technologies, but does this make their scholarship digital?

The word "digital" has become ubiquitous, but surprisingly many people are unable to provide a definition for the word "digital" and I often pose this question to both children and adults when discussing technology. Digital simply means that electric circuits in a device utilise pulses or signals which are either on or off using 5 volts or 0 volts. The utility of this is that these devices can be programmed as binary language forms the basis for other programming languages. My point here is that digital scholarship is not just scholarship when we use computers. Ayers (2013) brought some needed clarity here by stating that digital scholarship exists "to do things that simply cannot be done on paper" (p. 30).

This book is primarily about digital scholarship practice but terminology is an important part of this discussion. Chapter 1 builds on the term "Multimodal Theses and Dissertations" (MTDs) and recounts how a website was created to allow users to interact with explanatory animations made by children for the sake of their own learning. This was done for the Storyboard project (Jacobs, 2015) which was a PhD study conducted through the University of Melbourne. This chapter also looks at digital scholarship as a transdisciplinary practice to guide researchers and universities to navigate some of the technical and methodological issues involved when publishing an MTD. These issues are important but the formulation of the term "MTD" (Jacobs, 2018) might have been short sighted as researchers might want to conduct multimodal research and publish it on a dedicated website, but not for the purpose of acquiring a postgraduate qualification. This sets the scene for Chapter 2 to explore multimodal methods, regardless of whether a qualification is obtained as an outcome.

Chapter 2 introduces Provisional Multimodal Research (PMR) as a new research methodology. PMR is then contextualised by recounting the evolution of a longitudinal STEM integration project which involves codesigning integrated units of work using existing curriculum outcomes in primary schools from K-6. As this project is not being conducted to acquire a postgraduate qualification, the term MTD is not applicable although the multimodal practices involved are identical. Accordingly, PMR is the preferred term. This distinction is significant enough to have warranted PMR being part of the title for this book but the existing title, *Digital Scholarship in Education – Multimodality as a Window into Learning*, is best for presenting PMR as a niche practice within digital scholarship.

The power of naming things should not be underestimated. Papert (1996) noted this in his quest to describe the art of learning by saying, "A first step toward remedying these deficiencies is to give the missing area of study a name so we can talk about it" (p. 10). In recounting both the Storyboard project and the STEM project which inform this book, each project will also show how existing terminology was insufficient to accurately describe the methods and modalities pertaining to digital scholarship. Accordingly, PMR is an attempt to forge a path forward and lay the methodological groundwork for researchers who are constructing digital artefacts.

Chapter 3 presents an overview and guide for making and publishing your own website to embody multimodal research. A theme throughout this chapter is that you should aim to do most of the design work yourself, as having a firsthand knowledge of your website structure will surface the various technical, pedagogical and theoretical issues involved. Chapter 3 is also the chapter which links to the wider world of digital scholarship outside of education.

Chapter 4 provides a much-needed definition for digital pedagogy based around eight educational affordances of using digital devices, namely duplication, reversibility, iteration, collaboration, representation, dissemination, virtuality and searchability. By giving digital pedagogy a more specific yet inclusive meaning, these educational affordances are brought into the foreground to advance our understanding of learning in the digital era.

In summary, this book explores new methodological options which can improve both the visibility and quality of research. It does so by example using two case studies which have dedicated websites where readers can interact with the various elements of the research for themselves. This book also shows how the goals and affordances of digital scholarship can embody and present learning across the whole spectrum of education, from kindergarten through to postgraduate level and beyond. A book on digital scholarship may well be a contradiction in terms, but a definitive book on digital scholarship in education is long overdue.

## References

Ayers, E. L. (2013). Does digital scholarship have a future? *Educause Review*, *48*(4), 24–34. https://er.educause.edu/-/media/files/article-downloads/erm1343.pdf

Holdren, J. (2013, February 22). *Increasing access to the results of federally funded scientific research* [Memo]. Executive Office of the President. https://obamawhitehouse.archives.gov/sites/default/files/microsites/ostp/ostp_public_access_memo_2013.pdf

Jacobs, B. (2015). *Storyboard - Primary school children designing and making explanatory animations* [PhD dissertation website]. The University of Melbourne. https://brendanpauljacobs.com/

Jacobs, B. (2018, September). In search of the multimodal thesis. In *Eighth Annual Conference of the United States Electronic Thesis and Dissertation Association (USETDA)*. Denver. http://www.brendanpauljacobs.com/Jacobs2018.pdf

Papert, S. (1996). A word for learning. In Y. Kafai & M. Resnick (Eds.), *Constructionism in practice: Designing, thinking and learning in a digital world* (pp. 9–24). Lawrence Erlbaum Associates.

# 1 Multimodal theses and dissertations

## 1.1 Introduction

The opening sections of this chapter are based on a paper presented at the annual conference of the United States Electronic Thesis and Dissertation Association (USETDA) in September 2018 (Jacobs, 2018). The title of that paper was *In search of the multimodal thesis*, but there was a deliberate irony in that title as it was not really about trying to find a multimodal thesis, but rather, trying to write one. As part of my literature review about what had been done in this area, I conducted Internet searches periodically over a period of several years hoping to find an example which I could use as a precedent for my own research. Searching on Google for a "digital thesis" can provide access to millions of *digitised* theses, which are hardcopy theses that have been saved in a digital format such as PDF so that they can be archived and accessed online.

The terms "thesis" and "dissertation" are often used interchangeably to describe higher degree research publications. It is common in some countries such as the USA for "dissertation" to be reserved for doctoral work and "thesis" to describe master's level work. Multimodality is the existence and expression of meaning in multiple modes such as words and pictures but there is a much wider range of modes including gestures, body language and so on. Multimodality does not directly equate with multimedia as multimodality can be non-digital. Multimodality is also much wider than a web-based interface but hereafter, I will use the term "Multimodal Theses and Dissertations (MTD)" to refer to a web-based research publication as this is the specific practice which I will be discussing and critiquing. A close contender for a suitable term was "hypermedia thesis" as this describes web-based links to text and other media. The problem with this term is that digitised theses tend to be accessed through web browsers so searching for a hypermedia thesis is still not as specific as searching for a multimodal thesis. A candidate writing an MTD at either master's or PhD level will hereby be referred to as the "dissertator".

The precursor to the MTD is the Electronic Thesis and Dissertation (ETD). MTDs are more common in disciplines such as Arts and particularly in Media studies. The Networked Digital Library of Theses and Dissertations (NDLTD) recently marked their 20th anniversary of publishing and archiving research (http://ndltd.org) and first initiated annual awards for publishing ETDs in 2004. Ohiolink.edu has an ETD index to catalogue ETDs, often as a collection of files within a folder, which evolved from recommendations from the board's library committee back in 1987 (https://etd.ohiolink.edu). Although both of these sites have searchable databases, it is difficult to determine when the first multimodal PhD thesis in the field of education was published.

Foxton (2016) reported on a meeting held at the British library to discuss the possibilities and challenges involved with multimodal thesis publication, such as access and intellectual property. The perceived wariness on the part of academic committees and even PhD supervisors to embrace the world of multimodal research outputs has left libraries grappling with the same issues but without the direction and support that those at a higher-level in the university could be providing. Furthermore, Jubb (2017) noted that "Relatively few attempts have been made so far to exploit the potential of new technologies to challenge existing structures of scholarship; rather, the focus has been on replicating existing scholarly models" (p. 14). Other institutions beyond universities now share the responsibility for providing access to research such as the British Library who have demonstrated initiative and vision by collaborating with other stakeholders such as the Arts and Humanities Research Council (AHRC). Together they created the *Academic Book of the Future Project* which ended in 2016 after two years of consultation (Deegan, 2017; Jubb, 2017). The official report suggested that "to repurpose graduate training in line with new, non-print ecologies will require major change and investment" (Deegan, 2017, p. 31). My argument is not that we necessarily need to train researchers to use multimodal formats as, according to Deegan, only 1% of the multidisciplinary collection of over 5 million citations and 3 million full-text works indexed through the *ProQuest dissertations* and *Theses global service* contains any multimedia. My argument is that researchers who have multimedia as part of their research data should not have to face additional obstacles from universities when publishing their research.

The MTD discussed in this chapter is titled *Storyboard: Primary school students designing and making explanatory animations* (Jacobs, 2015). A non-university Uniform Resource Locator (URL) was used to provide access to this dissertation at http://www.brendanpauljacobs.com.

## 1.2 Constructionism

The theoretical framework for both the Storyboard project and the ongoing research which informs Chapter 2 is constructionism as articulated in Harel and Papert's seminal work from 1991. This framework is particularly useful for studies which revolve around the creation of an artefact to embody the learning. Harel and Papert (1991) first observed this over 30 years ago:

> They [the children] became software designers, and were representing knowledge, building models, and teaching concepts on their computer screens. They were thinking about their own thinking and other people's thinking – simultaneously – to facilitate their own learning.
>
> (p. 45)

Harel and Papert (1991) were among the earliest researchers to note that constructing digital artefacts is a multifaceted task stating that "The child-producer who wants to design a lesson on the computer must learn about the content, become a tutor, a lesson designer, a pedagogical decision maker, an evaluator, a graphic artist, and so on" (p. 78). Constructionism has been described in various ways as a learning theory, epistemology and theoretical framework, but the student-centred nature of constructionism made it a logical choice for the Storyboard project.

## 1.3 The Storyboard project

The Storyboard project (Jacobs, 2015) was a PhD research project conducted at the University of Melbourne. The eight participants in that action research study were girls and boys from grades five and six who chose their own topics and worked on their animations for one hour a week over a period of 17 weeks. As I was also the Performing Arts teacher, I already knew all 764 students at the school. The process of selecting the eight participants involved verbally explaining the project to the children and then waiting to see which ideas the children came up with for their proposed animation topics. Children who had workable ideas were then given Plain Language Statements and Consent Forms to take home to their parents as part of the ethics approval process.

### 1.3.1 Research question

The research question for the Storyboard project was, "In what ways can storyboarding and explanatory animation creation enable primary school students to articulate and consolidate their learning?" Figure 1.1 restates the research question diagrammatically. The two-way arrows were added during the data analysis phase when it became increasingly apparent just how intrinsic this connection was, particularly when the storyboard also functioned as a source for the animation imagery.

## 4  Multimodal theses and dissertations

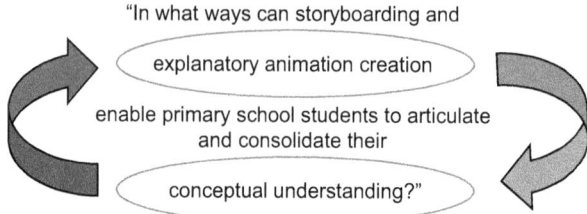

*Figure 1.1* Research Question for the Storyboard Project
Source: https://brendanpauljacobs.com/introduction.html (Used with permission).

### 1.3.2  Research methodology

Storyboard was a practitioner action research project that was documented as an explanatory case study. It also sought to utilise the dynamics of Vygotsky and Sakharov's dual stimulation method due to the close unity between conceptual tasks and their resolution. The dual stimulation method involves a problem-solving scenario where "the subject must be faced with a task that can only be resolved through the formation of concepts" (Vygotsky, 1987, p. 124). Vygotsky explained the nature of this link by stating that "the path through which the task is resolved in the experiment corresponds with the actual process of concept formation" (p. 128).

Daniels (2012) has further defined Vygotsky and Sakharov's dual stimulation method as an experimental approach where people are placed in a situation where "a problem is identified and they are also provided with tools with which to solve the problem or means by which they can construct tools to solve the problem" (p. 822). The first stimulus (i.e., problem) and the second stimulus (i.e., tools) are predetermined and so the point of this method is to understand the effect of the second stimulus on the first. In the Storyboard project, the first stimulus was the overall task of explaining a topic, and the second stimulus was the use of the evolving explanatory animation artefacts to embody the learning.

Although Vygotsky and Sakharov's dual stimulation method provided a dynamic approach for conducting the study, Cultural Historical Activity Theory (CHAT) provided both the vocabulary and perspective to understand conceptual change and artefact creation as recursive elements within a collaborative project environment. CHAT is based on the work of the Soviet researchers Vygotsky, Leontiev and Luria and further developed in the USA by Michael Cole, James Wertsch and others. Much of the international focus on CHAT today is due to the work of Yrjö Engeström and his sustained interest in activity. The notion of activity was particularly important for the Storyboard project because each of the students was required to perform a variety of technical and pedagogical roles as their explanatory animation creation task was clearly multifaceted. The multifaceted nature of the children's work was also captured in the 12 data collection methods.

### 1.3.3 Methods – Explanatory case study

This research project was titled "Storyboard" because I had already theorised that the content and order of the animation scenes could embody the learning. The animation platform that the Grade 5 and 6 students used was Microsoft PowerPoint because it was readily available and the students already had some familiarity with it. Additionally, the layout and design of the PowerPoint software itself was clearly influenced by the storyboard (Fleurke, 2011). The particular technique that was used, however, was initially unfamiliar to all of the participants. The various steps involved are described below:

1. Each student created their own PowerPoint file. A crucial part of the file management process was that each student saved their work with a different date-based file name each week. This simple practice of saving multiple versions of each student's work was vital as without this, there would not have been a data trail documenting all of their work.
2. Each student inserted combinations of auto shapes to construct their imagery and then created an identical copy of each slide (i.e., animation frame) by using the "Insert/Duplicate slide" command. Each successive frame was then manipulated by slightly moving the shapes and then this process was repeated.
3. When the slides were completed, the various animation frames were exported from PowerPoint using the command "Save as/Images/PNG". PowerPoint named each frame using sequential numbers.
4. Another PowerPoint slide (within the same file) contained the child's written explanation for the narration, which we called the voice-over script.
5. Each child read their voice-over script (i.e., narration) into a portable voice-recorder. These audio files were saved in MP3 format.
6. The final step involved importing all the images into video editing software (we used Adobe Premier Pro) and then synchronising these to the audio of the narration.

The multimodal nature of the explanatory animation creation task required 12 data sources to be generated throughout the Storyboard project. The students each produced three videos: (1) a prior knowledge video at the start of the project, (2) an explanatory animation at the end of the project and (3) a director's commentary about their animation to conclude the project. I kept daily reflections in my (4) reflexive journal and assessed the students after each session on a (5) conceptual consolidation rubric. I also wrote a (6) researcher reflection on each student each week and

6  *Multimodal theses and dissertations*

created (7) lesson plans for each session. Attendance was documented on an (8) attendance roll and the students and I also made video recordings of our (9) debriefing session at the end of the project. Component parts of the children's animations included their various (10) imagery files (i.e., PowerPoint files) and a (11) voice-over script that evolved during each session until it was eventually recorded as an audio file for narration purposes. The students also made audio recordings at the end of each session about their progress and plans as (12) weekly reflections that were later transcribed for closer analysis. These 12 data collection methods generated sufficient data to demonstrate that the power of the explanatory animation creation process is its ability to track and illustrate the conceptual-developmental pathway. Figure 1.2 illustrates the relationship between these sources and how the co-construction of the animation artefacts was

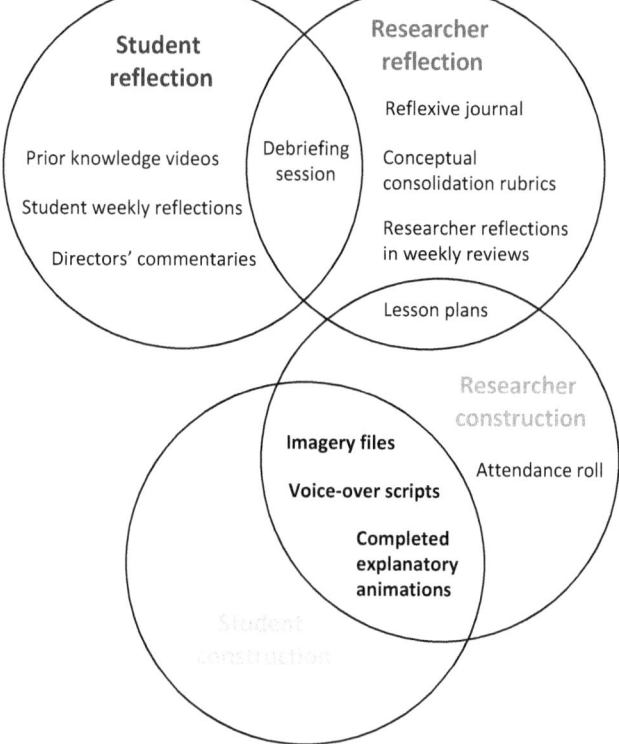

*Figure 1.2*  Venn Diagram of the 12 Data Sources
Source: https://brendanpauljacobs.com/methodology.html (Used with permission).

## Multimodal theses and dissertations 7

not a linear process but, rather, an interactive process. This Venn diagram also shows whether the data sources were primarily reflective (e.g., directors' commentaries) or constructive (e.g., imagery) in nature. Many thousands of files were created as each animation had component files such as images and audio recordings for narration. Although this research project was deemed to be low risk, it involved working with children and so it required separate ethics approval from both the Victorian Department of Education and Training and the University of Melbourne. The data sources listed in the consent forms allowed for the online publication of all imagery including videos, but pseudonyms were used to maintain confidentiality.

PowerPoint was chosen as the animation software as this was widely available and children had already discovered that they could create imagery using various auto shapes and then create frame-based animation by inserting duplicate slides and making small adjustments as an iterative process which soon generated hundreds of slides (i.e., frames). Each child changed the name of their work each week by simply adding the date into their PowerPoint files so as to preserve a digital chronology of their work as both process and product, with the product being the final animation artefact. Children also recorded directors' commentaries on their work and prior knowledge videos so a dedicated website (https://brendanpauljacobs.com/) was the most efficient way to link all of these files together. Back in 2015 it was still common to use a DVD to provide access to multimedia files to augment hard copies of PhD dissertations. The PhD was submitted for examination as bound hard copies with accompanying discs in accordance with university requirements. This was an inefficient way to interact with the content so the dedicated website was constructed in parallel with the hard copy version throughout the entire period of candidature, containing every word of the hard copy and using the same chapters and headings, and following all other academic conventions.

### *1.3.4 Data analysis and results*

Analysing the progress of each student was as an ongoing process where I sought to offer specific help for particular challenges throughout the 17 weeks of the project. Although some technical animation help was required, my primary role was in relation to the conceptual questions which the students had about their own content knowledge. Of all the 12 data sources shown in Figure 1.2, two were found to be particularly significant as follows:

1 What each student could articulate about their topic through their voice-over script.
2 What I knew about the topic as documented through my researcher reflections in weekly reviews.

8  *Multimodal theses and dissertations*

The grounds for comparison (i.e., why compare the children's voice-over scripts and my researcher reflections?) are based on the notion that storyboards are semiotic tools for cross-modal cognition (Jacobs et al., 2017). The term "cross-modal cognition" describes the ways in which learners in a multimodal environment creating explanatory animations are simultaneously working with different modalities, such as images and words, as different aspects of the same pedagogical task. The co-construction of knowledge as evidenced through the evolving digital artefacts also surfaced my own understanding of each topic. This provided a logical context for analysis as I would not have been able to make any judgements about each student's work without reference to my own understanding (Leite et al., 2007).

The iterative nature of learning is consistent with Vygotsky's (1978) notion of a zone of proximal development (ZPD) where a more experienced or knowledgeable helper, such as a teacher or parent, can provide targeted and personalised assistance to another person to facilitate learning. In the Storyboard project, the ZPD formed the frame of reference for ongoing comparisons between what each student knew about their chosen topic and what I knew as their helper. Through working with each of the eight participants, my own understanding of their particular topic was expanded in line with what John-Steiner (2000) described as "mutual zones of proximal development" (p. 177). To enter into the process of conceptual consolidation, it was necessary for me to grapple with the same conceptual issues as each of the students, which created an authentic context for the co-construction of knowledge embodied in the evolving animations.

## 1.4 The affordances of online publication

There were both anticipated and unanticipated benefits from compiling and presenting the Storyboard project as a multimodal dissertation. The anticipated benefits centred around the convenience of being able to view the content online. Of greater interest were three unanticipated benefits, namely the ability to include access to all of the data, the inclusion of digital appendices and the opportunity to observe patterns in the data that might not have been evident without the ability to scroll through pages. These three areas are interrelated but they can be described collectively as relating to the affordance of quality. Each area will now be discussed in turn.

### *1.4.1 Access to all of the data*

Corti and Fielding (2016) noted that "the ability to make data from a research study available via digital means is not just valuable as future-proofing but also for purposes of 'scientific transparency,' accountability, and integrity" (p. 8). They also suggested that "being able to directly examine the data that a researcher adduces in support of their analysis will inevitably change the ground of the epistemological debate" (Corti & Fielding, 2016, p. 11). The digital nature of the Storyboard project provided other researchers with the opportunity to confirm the data through the inclusion of hypertext links to the raw data. The inclusion of links to the children's PowerPoint files would not have been possible on paper due to the restriction of space. This augmented the referential adequacy and integrity of the research study, specifically in relation to confirmability. The chronological file-naming conventions used throughout the study also enhanced the methodological congruence through the creation of a logical framework for the data trail.

### 1.4.2 Digital appendices

The inclusion of digital appendices is also about accessing data, but this is nuanced with the opportunity to provide links to material which was not included in the original research design. For example, my researcher's reflexive journal ended up comprising an additional 40,000 words. Because the reflexive journal was compiled as a series of web pages where each month was on a separate page, it was easily included as links in a section titled "Digital appendices" (https://brendanpauljacobs.com/appendices.html).

### 1.4.3 Patterns in the data

Observing patterns in data can often lead to new insights beyond the scope of the original research question. In the Storyboard project, each child had their own page where all of the data was included in a large table where each week became a new row. The five columns were predetermined categories, namely:

- Audio files and PowerPoint files
- Transcripts (of student reflections)
- Voice-over scripts
- Researcher reflections
- Conceptual consolidation rubrics

These tables were too big for a traditional page of paper but the ability to scroll both up/down and left/right on a web browser made this data more manageable. One of the most significant insights from this research is that conceptual learning starts with using correct terminology to identify relevant components and then culminates in understanding the relationships between the components (Jacobs & Cripps Clark, 2018). This idea is developed further in Section 4.5.

The fact that each iteration of the children's work was also available on the website as links to the raw data was a methodological innovation. When students are creating digital artefacts which embody their own learning, the ability to refer to various versions of the source files can document a chronology of this learning which increases trustworthiness and Guba and Lincoln's (1999) other measures of credibility, transferability, dependability, confirmability and referential adequacy. The innovation is that these links do not take up actual space so the interconnectivity of an MTD presents new methodological options. Table 1.1 describes three affordances of online publication according to the particular practices involved.

Each of the three practices listed in Table 1.1 could be categorised as increasingly specialised examples of digital scholarship. For example, digital scholarship includes around 4.5 million ETDs as digitised PDFs in response to former US President Barack Obama's directive to make publicly funded research freely available (Holdren, 2013). Visibility is used here as a synonym for connectivity as people can access the Internet from classrooms across the education sector and also carry this option around with them through smartphones and other devices. The affordance of quality is reserved for MTDs as described above in relation to being able to observe patterns in the data. The final affordance of reference chronology involves archiving each iteration of a digital artefact. This theme is developed further in Chapter 2 as a new research methodology called "Provisional Multimodal Research (PMR)".

*Table 1.1* The Affordances of Online Publication

| Practice | Affordance | Explanation |
| --- | --- | --- |
| Digital scholarship | Visibility | ETDs and MTDs are available online. |
| Multimodal Theses and Dissertations (MTDs) | Quality | MTDs enable the dissertator to interact with the data in unique ways, which is likely to improve quality. |
| Provisional Multimodal Research (PMR) | Referential chronology | Having each iteration of an artefact enables the dissertator to document both the process and the product. |

## 1.5 The Networked Digital Library of Theses and Dissertations

An important organisation in the digital scholarship landscape is the Networked Digital Library of Theses and Dissertations (NDLTD, https://ndltd.org/). The call for papers for the *26th International Symposium of Theses and Dissertations* in 2023 (https://etd2023.inflibnet.ac.in/call_for_paper.php) used the following categories, which are also characteristic of the scope of their work:

- Managing ETDs
- ETD Metadata Lifecycle
- ETD and Open Science
- Research Data Repositories (RDRs)
- Bibliometric Analysis of FAIR ETDs
- Libraries Beyond Institutions
- ETD Meta Archive
- Analytics of ETDs
- Discoverability of ETDs
- Other Issues Related to ETDs
- Case Studies and Best Practices

As you can see, the focus is clearly on managing the logistics of ETDs. These are primarily digitised research outputs where the most common format is PDF.

## 1.6 The United States Electronics Thesis and Dissertation Association

The United States Electronics Thesis and Dissertation Association (USETDA) holds an annual conference where researchers and higher research degree administrators come together to discuss issues pertaining to ETD logistics and dissemination (http://www.usetda.org/). At the 2018 USETDA conference in Denver, the Storyboard project formed the focus of a presentation titled, *In search of the multimodal thesis* (Jacobs, 2018). This presentation explained how the search for a multimodal thesis was for the purpose of using any results as a precedent for a multimodal submission. As no examples had been found during my searches, I knew that it was possible that the Storyboard might actually be the first example in the field of education and this was subsequently confirmed by those in attendance at the conference. As my reason for finding a precedent had now come and gone, little more was done in this space other than the publication of *A transdisciplinary protocol for multimodal theses and dissertations* (Jacobs, 2021). This was published in the journal *Digital*

Scholarship in the Humanities because there was no journal for digital scholarship in education. The following sections restate and update the protocol.

### 1.7 A transdisciplinary protocol for digital scholarship

Do we really need a protocol for digital scholarship? A "protocol" is a procedure or system of rules to which various parties may choose to adhere. The transdisciplinary protocol in this chapter covers the logistical issues pertaining to the publication of MTDs. It is provided to help researchers to advocate their own path through the myriad questions, issues and obstacles around which many universities are currently grappling. (For technical guidelines about creating an MTD, see "Chapter 3: Guidelines for digital scholarship".) The protocol for digital scholarship outlined in this chapter is transdisciplinary because it provides a framework beyond the disciplinary perspectives. Figure 1.3 visually contrasts the various disciplinary approaches.

Jensenius (2012, para. 3) defined these categories as follows:

**Intradisciplinary**: working within a single discipline.
**Multidisciplinary**: people from different disciplines working together, each drawing on their disciplinary knowledge.
**Crossdisciplinary**: viewing one discipline from the perspective of another.
**Interdisciplinary**: integrating knowledge and methods from different disciplines, using a real synthesis of approaches.
**Transdisciplinary**: creating a unity of intellectual frameworks beyond the disciplinary perspectives.

The protocol described in the following section resonates more with the second part of the transdisciplinary description listed above. In other words, it is not so much a unity of intellectual frameworks but a

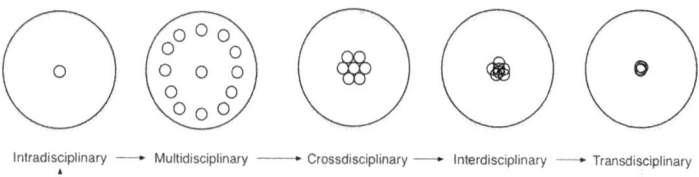

*Figure 1.3* Disciplinarities

Source: Alex Jensenius https://www.arj.no/2012/03/12/disciplinarities-2/ (Used with permission © 2012. This work is licensed under a CC BY licence.).

framework which is beyond the disciplinary perspectives. In this sense, digital scholarship is independent of any particular discipline. The point here is that the main priority for researchers is to contribute new knowledge to their particular discipline as the form of this knowledge is usually a secondary concern. This discussion will be continued in Chapter 2 (Section 2.2) in relation to form and function.

Multimodal publication is often perceived as being problematic with concerns about the logistics of accessing and archiving multimodal data. The following transdisciplinary protocol for digital scholarship was created to provide solutions to logistical issues which are then mapped to roles and responsibilities. The protocol is first presented as three statements and then each statement is extended with a brief discussion and rationale:

1 Location: Register your own Uniform Resource Locator (URL) after choosing a domain name.
2 Maintenance: The dissertator will write, link, upload and maintain all files to be accessed through a web browser.
3 Academic governance: A panel of university experts will assess the academic integrity of the MTD when the dissertator presents and defends their work.

*1.7.1 Location*

In terms of location, it is recommended that dissertators register, purchase and maintain their own URL. Some web creation sites provide free hosting, but there will be limitations on the domain name itself because it will usually require including the name of the provider in the actual name (e.g., www.wix.com/nameofdissertator). When a multimodal thesis is web based, the dissertator needs to develop the basic skills to put together the various pages which comprise the thesis in a web-based format such as HTML. It has been my experience that universities do not want to provide PhD candidates with File Transfer Protocol (FTP) access to upload content to the university's website so it is up to the author to obtain their own domain name and hosting to manage the site. Providing access to a multimodal thesis is then simply a matter of providing the reader with the URL of your website. Although this recommendation does not necessarily involve a digital object identifier (DOI), it does address the central issue for why DOIs were established in 2000 to provide a persistent identifier to ensure the longevity and reliability of web links. The location of MTDs appears to be the most contentious issue as registering a URL opens up additional issues around ownership, copyright, and intellectual property.

It is worth noting that the university website potentially could house MTDs as most existing Learning Management Systems (LMS) already provides multimodal creation and presentation functionality. Universities commonly pay for the LMS functionality that they require but the status quo in most institutions is currently inadequate for what MTDs require. For example, a digital portfolio commonly has a single page, or various sections on a handful of pages, but an MTD would generally have numerous pages linked together using names chosen by the dissertator instead of names generated by the LMS. For these reasons, many of the earliest examples of MTDs (primarily in the digital humanities) were originally located on each dissertator's URL and continue to be accessed from these same URLs. This is because a dissertator with their own URL will have maximum flexibility and efficiency during, and after their candidacy. In summary, there are two important advantages to having your own URL:

- No technical limitations for functionality
- Guaranteed ongoing access.

### 1.7.2 Maintenance

The dissertator will write, link, upload and maintain all files to be accessed through a web browser. They will also take responsibility for the ongoing functionality of the data. For example, shortly after submitting the Storyboard project for PhD examination in 2015, certain file formats such as flash video (.flv) were phased out meaning that they were no longer supported by web browsers. To keep the Storyboard site functional, I had to convert all videos to a more current format (namely.mp4), upload the new mp4 videos and change all pages that linked to the videos to include the updated file extensions. Such changes are not required very often, but it is unrealistic to expect anyone other than the dissertator to know that such changes are required and then to make the changes. It is also reasonable to assume that the dissertator would have the greatest interest in maintaining the functionality of the site because it showcases their research.

### 1.7.3 Academic governance

A panel of university experts will assess the academic integrity of the MTD when the dissertator presents and defends their work. This last part of the protocol might seem too obvious to list, but it raises an important point. By definition, new knowledge is new. According to Engeström (2001), when researchers are creating new knowledge "the object of activity is a moving target" (p. 136). By leaving the final determination about the academic quality and standards of postgraduate research until the end of a project, the dissertator will be able to present a more unified and persuasive account of the research than would have been possible at the start of a project. In other words, the existing conventions around confirmation of candidature near the beginning, and a dissertator defence towards the end, are sufficient to enable researchers to conduct their research without imposing additional hurdles throughout their candidature based on technological concerns. Most technological concerns are ultimately about formats or access and such issues invariably take care of themselves when emergent technologies mature and become mainstream.

Digital scholarship within education and digital humanities may differ with regard to word count requirements. Artefacts created in the digital humanities, such as choreographed dance performances, graphic novels or short films, are often considered to have met the word count requirements for a degree in recognition of the work that has gone into the creation of said artefacts, whether in part or in full. To my knowledge, the only extant example of digital scholarship in education is the Storyboard project, and that dissertation satisfied the original word count requirements without any reduction. However, this should not necessarily be taken as a precedent to restrict subsequent dissertators from receiving a reduction in their word counts. In summary, an MTD is an enhanced presentation format that uses a website to provide access to various media. The simple fact that websites use an index page as a main menu allows the user easy access to every file that the dissertator chooses to link. This means that the onus of dealing with folders lies with the dissertator rather than the user. "Chapter 3: Guidelines for digital scholarship" contains more information about managing this multifaceted process.

## 1.8 Theory in practice

The creation of an MTD is a multifaceted task. The Storyboard project was also a multifaceted task due to the different modalities involved in the explanatory animation creation task, namely images, written text, narration, colour, movement, metaphor, order, highlighting, spatial positioning, sounds effects and music. Perhaps this alignment is easiest to see when considering how the children's explanatory animation task literally embodied their learning. As noted in Jacobs (2020):

> How can one describe an explanatory animation without reference to the actual topic that comprises the subject matter? Likewise, how can one look at the conceptual ideas represented in animation without reference to the animation itself?
>
> (p. 60)

The link between theory and practice here is between the learning theory of constructionism and the children's explanatory animation creation task. Bereiter (2002) has reconciled even deeper epistemological issues inherent in design and learning by suggesting that improvement is a more fruitful attribute than truth:

> You cannot know or justify claim that you are getting closer to truth. That would require that you already have an idea of what the truth is. But you can specify ways in which one conceptual artifact is an improvement over its predecessor. You can show how it overcomes faults that were detected in the predecessor, how it accounts for facts that an older theory could not, or merely that it does the same conceptual job more economically or elegantly.
>
> (p. 429)

Bereiter's quest for improvement informed the Storyboard project as the children's explanatory animation creation process demonstrated instances of incremental improvement. These iterations documented the learning that was embedded in the children's conceptual artefacts as vivid examples of constructionist principles in action. For Sutter (2001), the challenge is for constructionists to explain how instruction fits with constructionist learning principles. Hoban et al. (2010) described constructionism as a "meta-theory" (p. 434) rather than an explicit learning theory. They also noted that there are very few studies using constructionism as a theoretical framework to "articulate the process of designing and making artefacts and justify why this process is beneficial for student learning" (Hoban et al., p. 435). Floridi (2011) articulated and expanded constructionist principles through his article *A defence of constructionism: Philosophy as conceptual engineering*. The six principles that Floridi presented are paraphrased in the following list:

1 The principle of knowledge – Only what is constructible can be known. (Anything that cannot be constructed, at least conceptually, can only be subject to working hypotheses).
2 The principle of constructability – Working hypotheses can be investigated through conceptual models and simulations.
3 The principle of controllability – Models must be controllable.
4 The principle of confirmation – Confirmation or refutation relates to the model itself rather than the system being modelled.
5 The principle of economy – The fewer resources used in a conceptual model the better.
6 The principle of context-dependency – Points of correspondence between simulation and simulated are local rather than global (pp. 300–301).

These six principles were applicable to the Storyboard project as the primary school children used conceptual modelling to enhance and expand their understanding. As Nersessian (2008) has noted, modelling has a "generative" quality (p. 48). It is the generative nature of the explanatory animation creation task which can lead towards conceptual consolidation.

## 1.9 Conclusion and recommendations

The Storyboard project demonstrated that explanatory animations can be authored by students for the sake of their own learning in contrast to the prevailing view where children are traditionally viewers of content created by professional animators (Jacobs & Robin, 2016). It is clear that the children's explanatory animation creation task was intrinsically multimodal as they were simultaneously dealing with various modes. Their imagery was qualitatively different from their text and so these images had to be handled differently. If words were used to describe the imagery without actually showing the imagery, it would have forced the reader to vicariously generate their own mental representations which would invariably be different from the children's own art. For these reasons, the multimodal nature of the dissertation provided a logical and vivid way to present the data. The digital nature of the children's animations also facilitated experimentation and duplication, and resonated with the work of constructionist researchers such as Resnick (2007) who noted:

> We never expect to get things right on the first try. We are constantly critiquing, adjusting, modifying, revising. The ability to develop rapid prototypes is critically important in this process. We find that storyboards are not enough; we want functioning prototypes.
>
> (p. 5)

The Storyboard project investigated the conceptual consolidation of primary school children through their creation of explanatory animations. It advanced our understanding of animation pedagogy and demonstrated how the children's mental models, as depicted through their animation key frames and storyboards, functioned as both flexible models and diagnostic tools.

My rationale for wanting to construct an MTD arose from an appreciation of the affordances inherent in the digital data generated by the eight Storyboard participants, giving full recognition to the richness of multimodality. The data collection was customised for my own research requirements and accordingly, any researchers who pursue MTD publication should use the most appropriate technologies for their own requirements. It is also worth noting that audio and video files are not necessarily a move away from written text as written text can actually enhance the functionality of such media. For example, it would have been easier to leave the spoken words from the children's reflections as audio files but, instead, they were also transcribed for closer analysis.

# 18  Multimodal theses and dissertations

Digital scholarship is not about the technology. Like all research, it is about the creation of new disciplinary knowledge so it should be no surprise that dissertators often seek to extend the boundaries of current practice. All research is unique, and so it is ultimately up to the dissertator to navigate the technical, ethical and logistical requirements of their dissertation. My hope is that this chapter can provide some guidance around the logistics of *how* and *why* when writing an MTD.

## References

Bereiter, C. (2002). *Education and mind in the knowledge age*. Lawrence Erlbaum.
Corti, L., & Fielding, N. (2016). Opportunities from the digital revolution: Implications for researching, publishing, and consuming qualitative research. *SAGE Open*, 6(4), http://dx.doi.org/10.1177/2158244016678912
Daniels, H. (2012). The interface between the sociology of practice and the analysis of talk in the study of change in educational settings. In J. Valsiner (Ed.), *The Oxford handbook of culture and psychology* (pp. 817–829). Oxford University Press.
Deegan, M. (2017). *The academic book and the future project report: A report to the AHRC and the British library*. https://academicbookfuture.files.wordpress.com/2017/06/project-report_academic-book-ofthe-future_deegan3.pdf
Engeström, Y. (2001). Expansive learning at work: Toward an activity theoretical reconceptualisation. *Journal of Education and Work*, 14(1), 133–156. https://doi.org/10.1080/13639080020028747
Fleurke, N. (2011). Imaging the storyboard: On networks, concepts and communication. *International Journal of the Image*, 1(3), 155–162. https://doi.org/10.18848/2154-8560/CGP/v01i03/44208
Floridi, L. (2011). A defence of constructionism: Philosophy as conceptual engineering. *Metaphilosophy*, 42(3), 282–304. https://doi.org/10.1111/j.1467-9973.2011.01693.x
Foxton, K. (2016). *Reasoning without words: Envisioning the multimodal thesis and its challenges*. https://academicbookfuture.org/2016/09/21/multimodal_thesis/
Guba, E. G., & Lincoln, Y. S. (1999). Naturalistic and rationalistic enquiry. In J. P. Keeves & G. Lakomski (Eds.), *Issues in educational research* (pp. 141–149). Pergamon.
Harel, I., & Papert, S. (Eds.). (1991). *Constructionism*. Ablex Publishing Corporation.
Hoban, G. F., Nielsen, W. S., & Carceller, C. (2010). Articulating constructionism: Learning science through designing and making "Slowmations" (student-generated animations). In C. H. Steel, M. J. Keppell, P. Gerbic, & S. Housego (Eds.), *Curriculum, technology & transformation for an unknown future - Proceedings of the 27th ASCILITE Conference* (pp. 433–443). The University of Queensland. https://www.ascilite.org/conferences/sydney10/procs/Hoban-full.pdf
Holdren, J. (2013, February 22). *Increasing access to the results of federally funded scientific research* [Memo]. Executive Office of the President. https://obamawhitehouse.archives.gov/sites/default/files/microsites/ostp/ostp_public_access_memo_2013.pdf

Jacobs, B. (2015). *Storyboard - Primary school children designing and making explanatory animations* [PhD dissertation website]. The University of Melbourne. https://brendanpauljacobs.com/

Jacobs, B. (2018, September). In search of the multimodal thesis. In *Eighth Annual Conference of the United States Electronic Thesis and Dissertation Association (USETDA)*. Denver. http://www.brendanpauljacobs.com/Jacobs2018.pdf

Jacobs, B. (2020). *Explanatory animations in the classroom: Student-authored animations as digital pedagogy*. Springer.

Jacobs, B. (2021). A transdisciplinary protocol for digital scholarship. *Digital Scholarship in the Humanities*, *36*(1), 115–221. https://doi.org/10.1093/llc/fqz087

Jacobs, B., & Cripps Clark, J. (2018). Create to critique – Explanatory animation as conceptual consolidation. *Teaching Science*, *64*(1), 29–39.

Jacobs, B., & Robin, B. (2016). Animating best practice. *Animation: An Interdisciplinary Journal*, *11*(3). 263–283. http://dx.do.org/10.1177/1746847716662554

Jacobs, B., Wright, S., & Reynolds, N. (2017). Reevaluating the concrete – Explanatory animation creation as a digital catalyst for transmediation. *Mind, Culture and Activity*, *24*(4), 297–310. http://dx.doi.org/10.1080/10749039.2017.1294181

Jensenius, A. R. (2012, March 12). Disciplinarities: intra, cross, multi, inter, trans [Blog]. https://www.arj.no/2012/03/12/disciplinarities-2/

John-Steiner, V. (2000). *Creative collaboration*. Oxford University Press.

Jubb, M. (2017). *Academic books and their futures: A report to the AHRC and the British library*. https://academicbookfuture.files.wordpress.com/2017/06/academic-books-and-theirfutures_jubb1.pdf

Leite, L., Mendoza, J., & Borsese, A. (2007). Teachers' and prospective teachers' explanations of liquid-state phenomena: A comparative study involving three European countries. *Journal of Research in Science Teaching*, *44*(2), 349–374. https://doi.org/10.1002/tea.20122

Nersessian, N. J. (2008). *Creating scientific concepts*. MIT Press.

Resnick, M. (2007, June). All I really need to know (about creative thinking) I learned (by studying how children learn) in kindergarten. In *Proceedings of the 6th ACM SIGCHI conference on creativity and cognition*, June 13–15, Washington, DC. ACM (pp. 1–6). https://doi.org/10.1145/1254960.1254961

Sutter, B. (2001). *Instruction at heart: Activity-theoretical studies of learning and development in coronary clinical work* [Doctoral dissertation]. Blekinge Institute of Technology. https://www.diva-portal.org/smash/get/diva2:838448/FULLTEXT01.pdf

Vygotsky, L. (1978). *Mind in society: The development of higher psychological processes*. Harvard University Press.

Vygotsky, L. (1987). An experimental study of concept development. In R. W. Rieber, & A. A. Carton (Eds.), *Collected works of L. S. Vygotsky* (Vol. 1, pp. 121–166). Plenum Press.

# 2 Provisional multimodal research

## 2.1 Introduction

The proverb, "necessity is the mother of invention" is as true today as when Plato made similar statements in *The Republic* or even earlier in Aesop's fable, *The crow and the pitcher*. This principle is also applicable to research methodologies as noted by Crotty (1998) who said, "In a very real sense, every piece of research is unique and calls for a unique methodology. We, as the researcher, have to develop it" (pp. 13–14). My research interests revolve around the creation of digital artefacts. This had necessitated the use of multimodal methods such as audio and video editing. Part of the rationale for formulating Provisional Multimodal Research (PMR) is so that I, and hopefully other researchers with similar interests, can focus on the findings and implications of research without having to spend additional time justifying points of departure from existing methodologies. Hyysalo et al. (2019) suggested that "every research design involves choices about where to address research effort" (p. 16). Perhaps the biggest departure is the idea of the purpose-built website, which is a unique contribution of digital scholarship although primarily evident in digital humanities.

PMR is a research methodology for educators which has been purpose built to document the process behind the construction of digital artefacts. The intrinsic strength of PMR is its ability to document change through the simple process of archiving files each time a change is made. These changes can be recounted when publishing and disseminating research through written text, annotated screenshots or even animations using video with explanatory narrations.

The chronology of digital files in PMR is a relatively recent possibility which continues an older debate about product v process. Kaplan (1964) suggested that the aim of methodology is to help us to understand the process of inquiry as an overarching goal beyond understanding the product. Büyükkarcı and Müldür (2022) investigated digital storytelling in

Provisional multimodal research 21

mathematics as a task for pre-service teachers. The participants documented the process in their reflective diaries and the product in their digital stories. Additional data took the form of structured interviews and focus groups. Interestingly, there was no chronology of the evolving digital stories through the use of version control. Different versions of the product can augment an understanding of the process by providing vivid examples of the actual artefact rather than vicarious descriptions of it. Contrasting product with process as intrinsically different things is really a false dichotomy as one is constrained by the other. This connection is also a common feature amongst evaluation studies (Hamza et al., 2020; Rosenblum et al., 2003).

## 2.2 Multimodality

Multimodality is a theory based on the recognition that there are many different modes that people use to communicate. According to Bernsen (2008), the basic notions of multimodality theory are "interaction, media, modalities, and information channels" (p. 6). A mode is a specific type of communication such as language, imagery or gesture. Kress (2010) has expanded the definition of "mode" to include attributes, such as colour. The commonality amongst modes is that they can convey meaning. The format in which a mode might be expressed, such as paper, email or text message, is referred to as the medium.

Mode and meaning have their origins in the notion of form and function which has informed an ongoing debate over many centuries. Sullivan (1896) coined the phrase "form ever follows function" (p. 407) but attributed the idea to the Roman architect Marcus Vitruvius Pollio. According to Andreou (2013), "in every attempt to communicate information the concepts of the medium and the message, form and content takes precedence" (p. 12). Ayers (2013) sees this as a missed opportunity in scholarship noting that "few scholars are trying, as they did earlier in the web's history, to reimagine the form as well as the substance of scholarship" (p. 28). Ayers (2013) also noted a disconnect here as "researchers routinely use electronic tools in their professional lives but not to transform the substance or form of their scholarship" (p. 26). The point is that the analysis of the form should begin with an analysis of the function. Kress and van Leeuwen (2006) were insightful here by stating that the person who makes a representation (i.e., sign-maker) displays their communicative interest through the "criterial aspects" (p. 7) evident in a depiction. Representations are value laden according to these criterial interests. "Representation is never neutral: that which is represented in the sign, or in sign-complexes, realizes the interests, the perspectives, the positions and values of those who make signs" (Kress & Mavers, 2005, p. 173). Jewitt

(2008) has also noted that mode and meaning are deliberately aligned when constructing multimodal texts:

> How knowledge is represented, as well as the mode and media chosen, is a crucial aspect of knowledge construction, making the form of representation integral to meaning and learning more generally.
>
> (p. 241)

The rise of multimodality has also led to new fields of study such as media archaeology which attempts to understand new and emerging media through a close examination of the past. Ibrus and Ojamaa (2020) have called for "greater interdisciplinary dialogue between media archaeology and cultural semiotics in order to understand the role of archives in facilitating communicative processes" (p. 49). Furthermore, they have noted that in this network era characterised by platforms such as YouTube, archives have become user-based rather than object-based. Websites play an interesting role as they are quintessential multimodal texts. As a medium, the Internet is growing exponentially in terms of the amount of available content, but it is also worth noting that part of this expansion involves the subsumption of other mediums such as DVD, CD-ROM, CD and even paper. Agre (1998) was insightful during the early stages of the Internet when he described it as a "meta-medium" noting that it is simultaneously a communications medium, computer system, discourse and set of standards.

Digital scholarship is a multimodal endeavour, but there is little in the way of theoretical overlap between digital scholarship and multimodality in the literature outside of the digital humanities. Perhaps the best way to introduce the issues pertaining to methodology, methods, data analysis and workflow using PMR is to contextualise this information in an example from an ongoing STEM integration study called the SILO project.

## 2.3 The SILO project

This section will outline the SILO project as a complete example of PMR. SILO is an acronym for Scientifically Integrated Learning Outcomes. It is also a play on words because education as a sector has often been criticised for teaching in silos where subjects are taught in isolation to each other. The aim of this research is to collaborate with teachers to develop and co-construct 28 units of work which cover the primary years using one unit for each term (i.e., 7 years × 4 terms = 28 units). The two research questions for the SILO project are:

1 How can the co-design of learning sequences and activities between teachers and researchers be effectively undertaken to improve the quality and usability of project findings and recommendations?
2 What might an integrated STEM curriculum for K-6 students look like?

*Provisional multimodal research* 23

A dedicated website has been created for the SILO project at https://silo.edu.au. The original methodology was Design-Based Research (DBR), but the reasons for changing methodologies are explored in Section 2.10.2.

The SILO project began in Queensland which is why the initial curriculum integration centred around the Australian Curriculum (Jacobs, 2022). I have since moved to NSW which has necessitated inclusion of the NSW Syllabus. The digital scholarship affordance of visibility was achieved by enabling teachers to access the website but the affordance of quality arose when a curriculum table was devised to compare and contrast the two curriculum documents. The curriculum mapping process did not lend itself to paper pages so the web-based table solution is a single html page with 29 rows and 5 columns (https://silo.edu.au/scopeandsequence.html). The 29 rows are for column headings and the names of each of the 28 units. The five columns are titled, "Year", "Name of unit", "NSW Syllabus", "Australian Curriculum" and "Learning intention". The learning intentions are my own paraphrases to draw out the essential STEM learning involved.

While scrolling through this table on the website, I came up with the idea of adding a sixth column titled "Scope and sequence". This new column was created to show where key concepts arise in a child's education relating to STEM. For example, in the first term of Foundation year, tables are introduced but graphs are introduced in the first term of Year 1. Variables are introduced in the third term of Year 2 and so on. This basic but important information is not condensed like this in either the NSW Syllabus or Australian Curriculum documents so this represents a positive step forward. The Education Council's (2015) *National STEM School Education Strategy 2016–2026* called for national collaborative actions such as these to "collect and develop online exemplar teaching modules, in partnership with university and industry, to assist in the delivery of best practice STEM teaching" (p. 8). Figure 2.1 shows the various data sources involved in the SILO project and how they can be categorised as being reflective or constructive in nature.

## 2.4 PMR methodology

The methods used in my previous work with Multimodal Thesis and Dissertations (MTD) in the Storyboard project often required explanation and justification for what, in essence, is simply a process where digital artefacts with an explanatory purpose are constructed over time (Jacobs, 2018). The term "MTD" has retained its original meaning in the literature but it is not directly applicable to the SILO project as this research is not being conducted in pursuit of a postgraduate research degree. Therefore, PMR retains the functionality and benefits afforded by MTDs but without

## 24  Provisional multimodal research

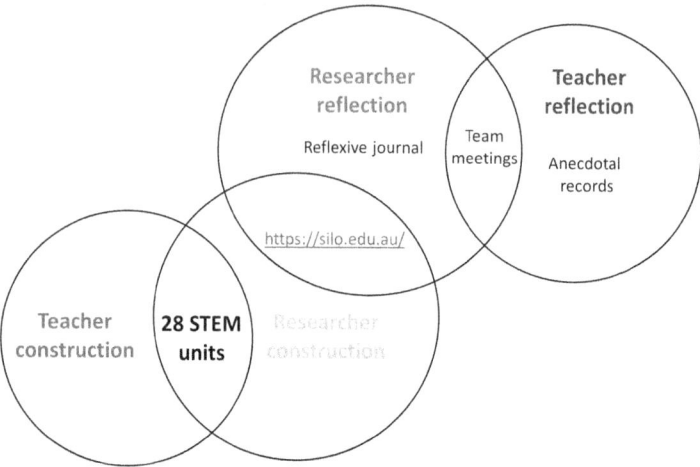

*Figure 2.1* Venn Diagram of the SILO Data Sources
Source: https://silo.edu.au/methodology.html (Used with permission).

restricting the purpose or intent of the researcher. There are three minimum requirements for PMR as follows:

1  The author of an explanatory artefact must be using digital tools in a digital environment.
2  Multiple versions of the artefact must be retained and archived, preferably after each significant iteration.
3  The rationale for changes must be documented. This usually takes the form of a reflexive journal to capture theoretical and pedagogical reasoning.

The digital environment sets the prerequisite condition, the multiple iterations provide the evidence base and the date-based rationale functions as a running commentary where emergent themes can be developed. This last point is important because the decision-making process recounted by the author of a digital artefact could be characterised as being subjective which is an issue pertaining to data analysis (see Section 2.7).

### 2.5  PMR methods

This section provides some guidelines for PMR in education but aims to remain broad enough for researchers who might use PMR in other contexts. An affordance of PMR is the ability to document change. The three distinctive elements in my initial use of PMR are:

1 Learning is embodied in an artefact. In the SILO project, the artefact could be seen as the website, but this can be further delineated into the 28 STEM units, and even the individual lessons or resources within each unit.
2 The status of provisional data.
3 The articulation of professional judgement.

To gain a clearer picture of PMR, it is important to look at the specific data collection methods which are characteristic of this approach, namely, the chronology of digital files and the researcher's reflexive journal.

### 2.5.1 Chronology of digital files

Digital files can refer to any file which is digital, but in the SILO project, the digital files are primarily the 28 HTML files which embody each of the 28 STEM units. All additional files such as images and videos are embedded into these 28 HTML files. In Chapter 3, Section 3.4.1 provides detailed examples of file management in digital scholarship, but the most important practice is to simply have multiple versions of each file by inserting the date into the file names.

### 2.5.2 Researcher's reflexive journal

Although my use of a journal started out as a reflective journal, I now refer to it as a "reflexive journal". Darling (1998) has articulated the differences as follows:

> Although reflection influenced the development of reflexive practice, there are profound differences. Reflexivity is proactive as its focus is on providing practitioners with a tool that will simultaneously improve their communication and help make them [be] aware of assumptions and priorities that shape their interaction with others.
>
> (para. 6)

A reflexive journal can be a source of data, but it can also contain instances of preliminary data analysis. Altrichter and Holly (2005) have noted how research diaries can include data, interpretation, commentaries and reflection. This promotes ongoing analysis, as "preliminary results of analysis can indicate which additional data are necessary to fill in the gaps in a theoretical framework and to evaluate intermediate results" (Altrichter &

Holly, 2005, p. 25). This is also in keeping with the nature of PMR where incremental improvements and refinements are made along the way. An example from my reflexive journal for the SILO project from March 7, 2023 is as follows:

> Today I swapped the order of SILO 3.3 "Coding" with SILO 3.4 "Questioning and predicting" so that the SILO 3.4 focus on hypotheses comes first. This is because the "if/then" nature of hypotheses can be also be applied to coding so this makes more sense in the overall scope and sequence.

That journal entry explained the rationale for the change, but there were other files impacted by the change namely:

- the Table of contents (https://silo.edu.au/toc.html),
- the Main menu for the 28 units (https://silo.edu.au/28stemunits.html),
- the colour-coded menu for the same 28 units which illustrates the main themes across the curriculum (https://silo.edu.au/spiralcurriculum.html),
- the Scope and sequence page (https://silo.edu.au/scopeandsequence.html) and
- the Discussion page (https://silo.edu.au/discussion.html).

More will be said about the researcher's reflexive journal in the following sections.

## 2.6 Referential chronology

In Chapter 1, there was some discussion around how quality and visibility are the two affordances of digital scholarship. PMR provides a third affordance, namely, "referential chronology" which is an extension of Lincoln and Guba's (1985) formulation of "referential adequacy". Referential adequacy involves archiving some of the raw data without analysing it. The existence of this unanalysed data could then demonstrate a researcher's confidence that this additional data could affirm the validity of their findings and reinforce the credibility of their whole approach.

PMR makes two important advances to referential adequacy. Firstly, the role of the researcher is quite different in PMR as they are the designer or co-designer of the learning artefact(s). This means that all of the data is analysed in real time whenever changes are made. The researcher's reflexive journal is the primary mechanism to document data analysis because a rationale is provided for each iteration of an artefact. The rationale for these decisions is archived in the chief investigator's data files rather than on the SILO website as teachers only want to see the latest versions. Secondly, the ease of duplicating digital files by either copying/

Provisional multimodal research 27

pasting/renaming or using "Save as" and then adding the new date means that this process can be easily managed. The archived data is available for further analysis but this is generally not required as the rationale for making changes has already been captured in the reflexive journal. These logistical differences are significant enough to warrant a new term for this process, namely, "referential chronology".

Referential chronology brings the subjectivity of the researcher into focus as an issue relating to dependability and how well a study can be replicated. Dependability itself, however, is more about the extent to which a researcher can account for the changing context during a study. Confirmability is often addressed directly after dependability as both issues deal with certification but in different areas of a study. "Confirmability shifts the emphasis from the certifiability of the enquirer to the confirmability of the data" (Guba & Lincoln, 1999, p. 147). Confirmability is an interesting element within PMR due to the intrinsically subjective nature of design. Another researcher could look at the chronology of my evolving artefacts and confirm that they understand the logic behind my rationale for any changes made, but this does not necessarily mean that they would have made the same decisions.

## 2.7 PMR data analysis

Teachers make countless decisions every day but, unlike researchers, the decision-making process which guides such decisions is rarely articulated. PMR seeks to elicit these decision-making processes by providing both the rationale for changes to an artefact and each version of the actual artefact. Data analysis in PMR occurs in real time whenever changes are made. The professional judgement of the researcher informs the changes, and the rationale for the changes is documented in a reflexive journal. Data is seen as provisional because each version of an artefact is a discrete source of data. The explanatory strength of PMR is achieved by capturing both the product and the process.

Data analysis in PMR blurs the boundaries between subjectivity and objectivity in a unique way due to the extensive evidence base which PMR generates. Definitions of subjectivity often relate to the lack of an evidence base but changes to an artefact in PMR are captured as written records of professional judgement. This principle also applies to tacit knowledge. Tacit knowledge is generally not written down or recorded but PMR can surface tacit knowledge as pedagogical and/or theoretical reasoning. According to Tripp (2012), it is "professional judgment which makes teaching a profession rather than a technically expert occupation or vocation" (p. 10). Tripp defined professional judgement as "those expert guesses which result from combining experience with specialist theoretical knowledge" (p. 7).

Professional judgement can be tentative when dealing with STEM education in primary schools because many teachers do not describe themselves as being competent in STEM knowledge or skills (Song & Zhou, 2021). This is an issue which has needed to be managed carefully in the SILO project because the evidence base for STEM is constantly changing and the role of the teacher should reflect the rapidly changing nature of STEM education. Methodologically, having such a high level of reliance on professional judgement is a deliberate choice to increase the frequency of research translation between myself as the chief investigator and the participating teachers. This grassroots approach was devised to integrate theory and practice and help ensure that each of the 28 STEM units is robust and workable. Ultimately, the teachers in the SILO project have the final say about what happens in their own classrooms and this cannot be overstated as the units of work must be feasible and fit for purpose.

## 2.8 The role of provisional data

A distinctive element of PMR is the role of provisional data. Instead of viewing provisional data as incomplete or as a placeholder for subsequent data, studies such as the SILO project see *all* data as provisional because the learning is ongoing and there is always room for further improvement. Such improvements might be related to artefacts at the lesson level, unit level or website level, all of which builds the knowledge base of the project as provisional data and reflection. As noted by Norum (2008), "artifacts become data through the questions posed about them and the meaning assigned to them by the researcher" (p. 245).

The word "provisional" has some negative connotations as this word is often used to describe a novice, such as a driver who has obtained a provisional licence indicating their lack of experience. Nevertheless, my use of the word in PMR is deliberate as I believe that change is inevitable in certain areas and that this has not been adequately theorised. For example, when we think of curriculum, we all know that it will change regardless of which country we live in or whether we operate in public or private institutions. We know this from experience and also by the fact that curriculum designers and administrators have full-time jobs for this very purpose. However, in many countries, updates to curriculum documents still occur as if these documents needed to be printed and published as hardcopy documents.

When I first became a teacher in 1999, I purchased the second iteration of the *Victorian Curriculum Standards Framework* for each of the eight key learning areas, complete with a ring binder, thinking that these would be my tools of the trade for the foreseeable future. The next iteration of the curriculum was subsequently made available as PDF documents which were freely available from the departmental website in 2006 as the

*Victorian Essential Learning Standards.* Across Australia to the current day, and in spite of the change from hard to soft copies, the publication process has not changed in terms of how long this process actually takes, which for some curriculum areas can be longer than others. Part of the reason for the slow rate of change is that there is often a period of consultation where teachers and parents can have their say about a draft curriculum before it is published. There is also an implementation timeline where schools have a transitional period before they are mandated to use the new curriculum. This example about curriculum is not strictly speaking about research data. The purpose of recounting this story is to suggest that the affordances of PMR, such as rapid updating and publication, can be utilised beyond research contexts. In such instances, I propose the term "provisional multimodality" to capture the affordances of PMR in instances where research is not being conducted.

Provisional data is also characteristic of open education. Traditionally, publication occurs when research is completed but, in my experience, publishing a draft version of research is the fastest way to keep it moving. Some researchers would not be comfortable working in this manner which is their choice. The provisional nature of the SILO project as an evolving evidence base is also in keeping with the nature of STEM where change is anticipated and welcomed.

In the SILO project, the notion of providing free resources was a secondary motivation. My primary motivation was to address the fact that it is very common for school curricula to mandate the component parts of STEM without actually having a STEM curriculum per se. This is also the case in Australia where all states follow the national curriculum and each have their own syllabi. This can be problematic as teachers are essentially left to make their own connections across the areas of Science, Technology, Engineering and Mathematics. According to Kelley and Knowles (2016), "in practice, STEM educators lack cohesive understanding of STEM education" (p. 1). The SILO project was designed to address this problem.

## 2.9 PMR practice

This section on PMR practice uses an autobiographical approach because I have devised this methodology myself. Accordingly, there are no other researchers currently using PMR for me to reference or mention at this time. However, my intention is to be descriptive rather than prescriptive as individual practices can, and should, vary according to context, experience and interests.

The workflow outlined below is specifically in relation to the SILO project. My daily practice using PMR revolves around the use of a reflexive journal with an entry for each day, seven days a week. These entries commonly start with, "Today I..." but unlike a memoir, these entries are not intended to be read one after another. Rather, they provide a reference and chronology of activity which can be used as an evidence base if required when publishing research findings.

An important additional affordance of the journal is that it can be used as a "to do" list where ideas are written with the knowledge that this file is reviewed on a daily basis. As such, some ideas are often just dot points. These ideas are not assigned to a particular date but, rather, placed at the bottom of the page as each HTML file within the reflexive journal covers an entire month. At the end of each month, a new file is created for the next month. Any ideas which have not been actioned are copied over to the next month so that they are not forgotten. To keep formatting and naming consistent, I always create the next month by "saving as" from the old file. For example, "september2023.html" becomes "october2023.html" and then the September entries are deleted from the October file leaving the "to do" items at the bottom unchanged.

Further reflection on the use of the journal has led to a recent breakthrough in my own understanding of the "to do list". When I first started writing about the list, I had made an assumption that the various items were tasks to be done and that my ultimate goal was to action them all as I worked my way through the list. Perhaps this was due to my preference to keep my email inbox clear through the extensive use of subfolders so that nothing remains in the inbox for more than a day or so. As much as I try, there always seems to be between 10 and 20 items on my "to do list" for the SILO project. The breakthrough in my thinking is the realisation that I can continue my research each day referring to an optional list of items to work on from this list. The benefit of this approach is that I never get stuck for ideas or fall into procrastination.

A final point about the journal is that it can be used for forward planning purposes too. For example, I was recently contacted by a teacher from the pilot school for the SILO project. This teacher wanted me to know in advance that I would have her 5/6 composite class for the first two hours when I next visited the school. I then added some activities to my journal for that date so that I had a record of it. The fact that this was actually written on Thursday 18th May rather than Tuesday 23rd May was not important.

Although the SILO project is the only extant example of PMR, some of the methods and practices involved were foreshadowed in the Storyboard project. However, the Storyboard and SILO projects had significant differences in four areas as indicated in Table 2.1.

The differences outlined in Table 2.1 show that PMR does not require online access to all files. Multiple versions of the artefacts and regular journal entries are basic components of the PMR methodology, but there is no requirement to provide open access to all of these files. Referential chronology can still be maintained without open access as this data still exists offline and can be accessed as required by the researcher.

*Table 2.1* Variations in PMR Practice

|  | Storyboard project | SILO project |
|---|---|---|
| **Purpose** | PhD qualification | Research interest |
| **Duration** | Fixed term | Ongoing |
| **Reflexive journal** | Available online | Not available online |
| **Online access** | All versions of all files | Only the most recent versions of certain files |

## 2.10 Critiquing PMR

This section will explore the types of claims which can be made using PMR and the relationship between data and research. Research methodologies are variously described in relation to being qualitative, quantitative or a combination of approaches according to the data which might be collected or generated in a study. According to the US Department of Health and Human Services (2009), the "Common Rule" defines research as "a systematic investigation, including research development, testing and evaluation, designed to develop or contribute to generalizable knowledge" (§ 46.102). Ethics approval within disciplines such as education often use terminology from health settings due to the commonality of having human participants. The Office of Research Integrity (n.d.) provides additional clarification by stating that a project or study can be classified as research if it:

- is conducted with the intention of drawing conclusions that have some general applicability and
- uses a commonly accepted scientific method.

The burden of proof to provide a "commonly accepted scientific method" might seem arduous when introducing a new research methodology but there are other definitions which are more appropriate for research in education. According to the Australian Research Council (2015), "research is defined as the creation of new knowledge and/or the use of existing knowledge in a new and creative way so as to generate new concepts, methodologies, inventions and understandings" (p. 3).

The bigger issue is in relation to whether research findings should be generalisable. Guba and Lincoln (1999) addressed this issue many years ago in their discussion of transferability. Transferability relates to the possible extent that elements from a study might reasonably be transferred to other settings. Guba and Lincoln (1999) proposed that researchers provide a detailed and sufficiently thick description to the extent that others might be afforded a "vicarious experience of it" (p. 148). The purpose of the vicarious experience is to enable others to make judgements about a study, particularly about the researcher's working hypotheses, which might be transferable to another context. Even earlier than this, Lincoln and Guba (1985) described transferability in relation to a transfer between the "sending" and "receiving" contexts and further noted that "transferability inferences cannot be made by an investigator who knows *only* the sending context" (p. 297 original emphasis). Establishing the feasibility for transferability then becomes the responsibility of the researcher in the receiving context as "the burden of proof lies less with the original investigator than with the person seeking to make an application elsewhere" (Lincoln & Guba, 1985, p. 298). It is no exaggeration to say that Lincoln and Guba significantly raised the status of qualitative research by questioning the whole notion of generalisability. By putting the burden of proof back on the receiving context, they were essentially saying that qualitative researchers need not concern themselves with generalisability. To reinforce this point, I will restate the two research questions from the SILO project in relation to generalisability:

1 *How can the co-design of learning sequences and activities between teachers and researchers be effectively undertaken to improve the quality and usability of project findings and recommendations?*
   The model which we adopted where I did all of the website development in response to feedback from teachers was a logistical choice to keep the project moving. This worked well for us, and might be of interest to others, but we are not saying that others must work in this manner.
2 *What might an integrated STEM curriculum for K-6 students look like?*
   It is this second question which best demonstrates PMR in action. The SILO website shows exactly what an integrated STEM curriculum *might* look like, but the word "might" implies that it could look very different depending on the context of other schools in other countries.

Critiquing PMR can also help locate this emerging methodology in relation to other comparable research methodologies. The focus on artefact development in PMR has some relevance to the biographies of artefacts and practices (BOAP) framework. However, as noted by Hyysalo et al. (2019), there are at least eight key principles and concepts which "should be seen as minimal inclusion criteria" (p. 6). Many of these such as attending to the detailed dynamics of sociotechnical change are simply not relevant to PMR and the BOAP framework often seeks to understand the dynamics between the artefact creator and end user. This distinction is blurred when the creator and end user are the same person so perhaps an "autobiography" of artefacts and practices framework would be more relevant.

The three research methodologies which are most relevant to PMR are practitioner action research, Design-Based Research (DBR) and autoethnography. Action research gives full consideration of the context, setting and proximity of all stakeholders, but the hallmark of action research is change. This emphasis on change resonates with DBR, and the dynamics of self-awareness during the design process are reminiscent of autoethnography. Ultimately, the following discussion will show that these three methodologies are not inadequate or insufficient for conducting studies such as the SILO project, but that the particular methods used in PMR are fit for purpose and well positioned to capture generative praxis.

### 2.10.1 Practitioner action research

Practitioner action research is primarily undertaken by teachers who are researching interventions within their own schools. However, Eikeland (2012) was cautionary about deemphasising the practitioner orientation as a mere checklist for place of employment as practitioner action research should be primarily concerned with generating new praxis. According to Somekh and Lewin (2005), "praxis refers to the process of embedding the development of theory in practical action" (p. 347). It is worth noting that the Storyboard project (Jacobs, 2015) was conducted as practitioner action research but this was done many years before PMR was articulated. Figure 1.1 in Chapter 1 outlined the 12 data sources used in that study, of which the date-based versions of the evolving artefacts and reflexive journal entries were of vital importance. As the data collection phase was conducted in 2011, it is understandable why the idea of proposing a new research methodology never occurred to me as a PhD student in the early stages of my candidature.

### 2.10.2 Design-Based Research (DBR)

Some further comments about PMR are required in relation to why it was necessary to depart from DBR for the SILO project. Sandoval and Bell (2004) noted that the evolving design of the research constitutes a distinct source of data which was a key consideration as change was not only anticipated but welcomed. Sandoval (2014) further noted that there is no clearly identifiable set of methods that can be labelled as DBR and that the commonality is mainly in terms of certain commitments that include "the joint pursuit of practical improvement and theoretical refinement; cycles of design, enactment, analysis, and revision; and attempts to link processes of enactment to outcomes of interest" (pp. 19–20). Sandoval's main contribution here is what he calls "conjecture mapping", which involves articulating and testing opinions or conclusions formed on the basis of incomplete information. In this sense, conjecture mapping could be likened to "hypotheses about how learning happens in some context and how to support it" (Sandoval, 2014, p. 20). Accordingly, the working hypothesis for the SILO project can be stated as follows: if students and teachers have a daily STEM focus, they will expand their STEM knowledge and skills. The primary appeal of DBR was the importance given to interventions in classroom settings and the fact that the evolving plans constituted a distinct source of research data.

Reeves (2006) was influential in the evolution of DBR by articulating four distinct phases, namely analysis, development of solutions, iterative cycles of testing and reflection. These four elements were evident in the SILO project, but not in the discrete linear manner which Reeves proposed. In the SILO project particular components of a lesson sequence, such as the inclusion of a new video, might involve the selection, embedding and testing of the video, but these activities generally occur during the same editing session. For example, this editing work might only involve only one of the 28 SILO units leaving the others unchanged. In this way the four phases were never applied to the whole SILO project. Similarly, although the SILO project has end dates for the various ethics approvals, these will be renewed and the website will be continually refined as this project is longitudinal and the plan is that this research will be ongoing.

### 2.10.3 Autoethnography

Autoethnography is an autobiographical genre of qualitative academic writing that draws on the lived experience of the author. According to Poulos (2021), autoethnography "attempts to recenter the researcher's experience as vital in and to the research process" (p. 4). Autoethnographers can access a wide range of data gathering and research tools including artefact analysis and journaling. Although these two particular components are also evident in PMR, there are some fundamental differences in relation to process and product. An intrinsic strength of autoethnography is the ability to document first-hand accounts of change, although this might not involve a product or artefact. The centrality of artefact creation is more characteristic of arts-based research.

### 2.10.4 Arts-based research

Arts-based research has some obvious parallels with PMR as it is quite common for academics in the arts to research their own process throughout the creation of artefacts. Mäkelä (2007) spoke of "knowing through making" (p. 157) and the role of the artefact in practice-led research. The parallels with the arts-based research and PMR are clearly evident and perhaps my own background as a performing arts teacher might have led me down this path subconsciously before my transition into academia.

The commonality between the arts and PMR is even stronger when considering the wider concept of *design*. Simon (1969) proposed this back in the late 1960s as the "science of design" as he found common ground across the arts, sciences and technology as an interdisciplinary field. For this reason, I originally theorised PMR as being interdisciplinary but I now see it as transdisciplinary because some of the insights gained from multimodal immersion can transcend individual disciplines. The following section on the design cycle demonstrates how the iterative nature of PMR can lead to insights when assembling research data as an evolving website.

## 2.11 The design cycle

As teachers we often revisit topics throughout the primary years with increasing complexity. We do this because it suits the age group we are working with and because the curriculum is also constructed using this approach. An example of this is when children write increasingly sophisticated fictional stories throughout their primary years. Bruner (1960) proposed that topics can be revisited at higher levels of complexity which is why this approach is known as the "spiral curriculum". The same approach can also be applied to emerging topics which are not clearly articulated in the curriculum such as STEM education.

Bruner's approach has become widely influential based on his hypothesis that any subject "can be taught effectively in some intellectually honest form to any child at any stage of development" (1960, p. 33). Within the very same paragraph, Bruner stated that, "No evidence exists to contradict it; considerable evidence is being amassed which supports it" (p. 33). Over 60 years later this is still largely the case. Figure 2.2 is an example from the SILO project of the spiral curriculum applied to the design cycle.

The design cycle is an important STEM concept. The formulation of "Think, Make, Improve" (TMI) is from Martinez and Stager (2013) who proposed that "reducing the process to three steps minimises talking and maximises doing" (p. 54). TMI is also an example of the maxim to "make everything as simple as possible but not simpler" which is widely attributed to Albert Einstein. The expanded language for Year 2 is from the Australian Curriculum, namely "Investigating and defining", "Generating and designing", "Producing and implementing", and "Evaluating" (Australian Curriculum, Assessment and Reporting Authority [ACARA], 2022). The Year 4 version retains the previous versions but with the additional dynamics introduced in the Stanford design cycle (Shanks, 2010)

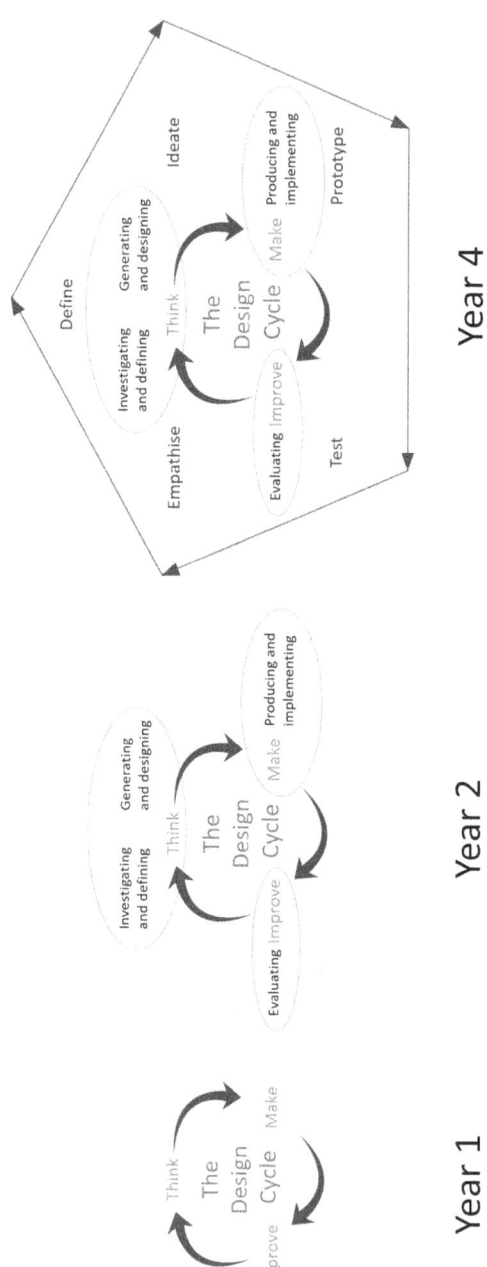

*Figure 2.2* The Expanded Design Cycle
Source: https://silo.edu.au/literature.html (Used with permission).

which adults use to identify commercial opportunities and develop new products, namely:

- Empathise
- Define
- Ideate
- Prototype
- Test.

The point here is that the previous versions of the design cycle are not changed but, rather, expanded. This is because prior knowledge can be built upon. Prior knowledge is not like scaffolding which is generally removed or replaced. Bruner did not specify a particular interval for when to revisit a topic. This is likely because each topic is different so the spiral curriculum can be utilised on a case-by-case basis.

## 2.12 Conclusion and recommendations

Researchers who conceptualise their research as fully digital, multimodal constructions such as dedicated websites, can let the research evolve to become fit for purpose, taking its own shape as generative praxis. Due to the additional time required to generate, curate and present multimodal data, researchers should only consider using PMR if they are working with data which is intrinsically digital, rather than data which has been digitised.

A recommendation which other researchers could explore in relation to PMR practice is the juxtaposition of material for different contexts. For example, each of the 28 STEM units in the SILO project is independent of who the viewer/user is. If there was a need to differentiate the content for pedagogical or regional reasons, it would be relatively easy to enable this through the use of sub folders to create different versions of each STEM unit with differing complexity. There has yet to be a reason for me to do this, but this would create some interesting new dynamics for other researchers who might benefit from this approach. The use of commentaries also provides additional functionality which researchers could utilise on their websites. This could be achieved in a variety of ways such as hover text or as links to additional sections to go more deeply into a discussion.

The main strength of PMR is in the abundance of digital data documenting the construction process, but researchers must be diligent, consistent and logical with their file naming and saving conventions. Ultimately, it is the quality of the reflections made to justify the rationale for each iteration and change which makes PMR unique as the data analysis occurs concurrently with the construction of an artefact. Animators, video editors, audio engineers, graphics designers and other creative professionals make countless decisions on a daily basis, but these decisions are intrinsically pedagogical when the media has an explanatory purpose. Future applications of PMR could involve Content Management Systems (CMS) and Learning Management Systems (LMS) due to the iterative nature of units within university courses and the need for continual improvement.

The issue of whether PMR necessarily requires the use of a dedicated website is yet to be determined, but the single extant example provided by the SILO project suggests that it does. This would further distinguish PMR as a specific methodology for research projects where the central focus is the development of digital artefacts, including websites as the quintessential multimodal artefact.

## References

Agre, P. (1998). The internet and public discourse. *First Monday*, *3*(2). https://doi.org/10.5210/fm.v3i2.581

Altrichter, H., & Holly, M. L. (2005). Research diaries. In B. Somekh, & C. Lewin (Eds.), *Research methods in the social sciences* (pp. 24–32). SAGE.

Andreou, A. P. (2013, October). Conceptual metaphors as image schemas in information visualizations. In *2CO Communicating complexity: 2013 Conference Proceedings* (pp. 12–18). Edizioni Nuova Cultura, University of Sassari. http://www.2coconference.org/docs/2CO_book_light_bn.pdf

Australian Curriculum, Assessment and Reporting Authority. (2022). *Australian Curriculum: Design and Technologies* (Version 9.0). https://v9.australiancurriculum.edu.au/

Australian Research Council. (2015). *2015–2016 State of Australian university research Volume 1 ERA national report*. Australian Government. https://www.arc.gov.au/sites/default/files/minisite/static/4551/ERA2015/downloads/ARC03966_ERA_ACCESS_151130.pdf

Ayers, E. L. (2013). Does digital scholarship have a future? *Educause Review*, *48*(4), 24–34. https://er.educause.edu/-/media/files/article-downloads/erm1343.pdf

Bernsen, N. O. (2008). Multimodality theory. In D. Tzovaras (Ed.), *Multimodal user interfaces: From signals to interaction* (pp. 5–29). Springer. https://doi.org/10.1007/978-3-540-78345-9_2

Bruner. J. (1960). *The process of education*. Harvard University Press.

Büyükkarcı, A. & Müldür, M. (2022). Digital storytelling for primary school mathematics teaching: Product and process evaluation. *Education and Information Technologies*, *27*(4), 5365–5396. https://doi.org/10.1007/s10639-021-10813-8

Crotty, M. (1998). *The foundations of social research*. Allen & Unwin.

Darling, I. (1998). *Action evaluation and action theory: An assessment of the process and its connection to conflict resolution* [Web page]. http://www.lupinworks.com/ar/Schon/Paper6.html

Education Council (2015). *National STEM School Education Strategy 2016–2026*. https://www.dese.gov.au/download/12532/national-stem-school-education-strategy/23618/national-stem-school-education-strategy/pdf

Eikeland, O. (2012). Action research - Applied research, intervention research, collaborative research, practitioner research or praxis research? *International Journal of Action Research*, *8*(1), 9–44. https://nbn-resolving.org/urn:nbn:de:0168-ssoar-371155

Guba, E. G., & Lincoln, Y. S. (1999). Naturalistic and rationalistic enquiry. In J. P. Keeves, & G. Lakomski (Eds.), *Issues in educational research* (pp. 414–449). Pergamon.

Hamza, D. M., Ross, S., & Oandasan, I. (2020). Process and outcome evaluation of a CBME intervention guided by program theory. *Journal of Evaluation in Clinical Practice*, *26*(4), 1096–1104. https://doi.org/10.1111/jep.13344

Hyysalo, S., Pollock, N., & Williams, R. (2019). Method matters in the social study of technology: Investigating the biographies of artifacts and practices. *Science & Technology Studies*, *32*(3), 2–25. https://doi.org/10.23987/sts.65532

Ibrus, I., & Ojamaa, M. (2020). The creativity of digital (audiovisual) archives: A dialogue between media archaeology and cultural semiotics. *Theory, Culture & Society*, *37*(3), 49–70. https://doi.org/10.1177/0263276419871646

Jacobs, B. (2015). *Storyboard - Primary school children designing and making explanatory animations* [PhD dissertation website]. The University of Melbourne. https://brendanpauljacobs.com/

Jacobs, B. (2018, September). In search of the multimodal thesis. In *Eighth Annual Conference of the United States Electronic Thesis and Dissertation Association (USETDA)*. Denver. http://www.brendanpauljacobs.com/Jacobs2018.pdf

Jacobs, B. (2022). Improving primary STEM education by integrating the Australian Curriculum. *Curriculum Perspectives*, https://doi.org/10.1007/s41297-022-00163-x

Jewitt, C. (2008). Multimodality and literacy in school classrooms. *Review of Research in Education*, *32*(1), 241–267. https://doi.org/10.3102/0091732X07310586

Kaplan, A. (1964). *The conduct of inquiry: Methodology for behavioural science*. Chandler Publishing Company.

Kelley, T. R., & Knowles, J. G. (2016). A conceptual framework for integrated STEM education. *International Journal of STEM education*, *3*(1), 1–11. https://doi.org/10.1186/s40594-016-0046-z

Kress, G. (2010). *Multimodality - A social semiotic approach to contemporary communication*. Routledge.

Kress, G., & Mavers, D. (2005). Social semiotics and multimodal texts. In B. Somekh, & C. Lewin (Eds.), *Research methods in the social sciences* (pp. 172–179). SAGE.

Kress, G., & van Leeuwen, T. (2006). *Reading images: The grammar of visual design* (2nd ed.). Routledge.

Lincoln, Y., & Guba, E. (1985). *Naturalistic inquiry*. SAGE.

Mäkelä, M. (2007). Knowing through making: The role of the artefact in practice-led research. *Knowledge, Technology & Policy*, *20*, 157–163. https://doi.org/10.1007/s12130-007-9028-2

Martinez, S. L., & Stager, G. (2013). *Invent to learn*. Constructing Modern Knowledge Press.

Norum, K. E. (2008). Artifact analysis. In L. M. Given (Ed.), *The Sage encyclopedia of qualitative research methods* (pp. 24–25). Sage publications.

Office of Research Integrity. (n.d.). *Chapter 3. The protection of human subjects (Definitions)*. Retrieved August 8, 2023 from https://ori.hhs.gov/content/chapter-3-The-Protection-of-Human-Subjects-Definitions

Poulos, C. N. (2021). *Essentials of autoethnography*. American Psychological Association.

Reeves, T. (2006). Design research from a technology perspective. In J. Van den Akker, K. Gravemeijer, S. McKenney, & N. Nieveen (Eds.), *Educational design research* (pp. 52–66). Routledge.

Rosenblum, S., Weiss, P. L., & Parush, S. (2003). Product and process evaluation of handwriting difficulties. *Educational Psychology Review*, *15*(1), 41–81. https://doi.org/10.1023/A:1021371425220

Sandoval, W. A. (2014). Conjecture mapping: An approach to systematic educational design research. *Journal of the Learning Sciences*, *23*(1), 18–36. https://doi.org/10.1080/10508406.2013.778204

Sandoval, W. A., & Bell, P. (2004). Design-based research methods for studying learning in context: Introduction. *Educational Psychologist*, *39*(4), 199–201. https://doi.org/10.1207/s15326985ep3904_1

Shanks, M. (2010). *An introduction to design thinking – Process guide*. Hasso Plattner Institute of Design at Stanford. https://web.stanford.edu/~mshanks/MichaelShanks/files/509554.pdf

Simon, H. (1969). *The sciences of the artificial*. The MIT Press.

Somekh, B., & Lewin, C. (Eds.). (2005). *Research methods in the social sciences*. SAGE.

Song, H., & Zhou, M. (2021). STEM teachers' preparation, teaching beliefs, and perceived teaching competence: A multigroup structural equation approach. *Journal of Science Education and Technology*, *30*(3), 394–407. https://doi.org/10.1007/s10956-020-09881-1

Sullivan, L. H. (1896). The tall office building artistically considered. *Lippincott's Magazine*, *57*(March), 403–409. https://openlibrary.org/books/OL24600425M/The_tall_office_building_artistically_considered

Tripp, D. (2012). *Critical incidents in teaching: Developing professional judgement* (Classic edition). Routledge.

US Department of Health and Human Services. (2009). *Protection of human subjects*. 45 CFR § 46.102. https://www.hhs.gov/ohrp/regulations-and-policy/regulations/45-cfr-46/index.html

# 3 Guidelines for digital scholarship

## 3.1 Introduction

Digital scholarship is variously defined as the publication of master's theses and doctoral dissertations in a digital medium. This practice has been around in the humanities for over 20 years and is generally centred around a creative artefact which is often given special consideration towards the required wordcount. Ayers (2013) provided a more concise definition for digital scholarship as "discipline-based scholarship produced with digital tools and presented in digital form" (p. 24). While digital tools and technologies have given many of us the opportunity to increase our online presence and participation, academia has evolved alongside this new reality in interesting ways. Weller (2018) is insightful here by concluding that:

> What has been realised then is not so much a revolution in academic practice, but a gradual acceptance and utilisation of digital scholarship techniques, practices and values. This means that depending on your particular perspective, it can seem to be simultaneously true that radical change has taken place, and nothing has fundamentally altered.
> (p. 63)

Murphy and Costa (2019) suggested that digital scholarship and the association of new technologies with scholarly activity is more than simply a process of digitising academic content, as "it marks a new shift in academic practice from a formal, one-dimensional type of communication to different forms of engagement with academic knowledge within and beyond the academy" (p. 208). However, even more transformative than the potential forms of engagement with others is the fact that the author of a digital scholarship publication engages with their own content as a designer, coder and proof reader. This provides opportunities to gain insights which can be generative for new disciplinary knowledge due to sustained, multimodal immersion.

The dynamics involved in the artefact construction process first became apparent to me during my master's degree (Jacobs, 2007). My research at that time sought to explore animation as a medium to teach musical theory to six of my teaching colleagues at a primary school who described themselves as "non-musical". The master's degree was titled *Animating best practice*, but a potential obstacle encountered during the early stages of that research had a profound impact on the quality of the research and eventually led to my transition from primary school teaching to academia. The obstacle was that I had originally planned to design the animations and have some animation students at the same university actually make the animations. It took quite some time to get a definitive answer about my request but the end result was that I was on my own as no students were interested in such a collaboration.

My next course of action was to meet with a professional animator to discuss the project. Towards the end of that meeting, he informed me that I could not afford him based on the number of animations and amount of collaboration required. He was very insightful when he explained that animators make countless decisions. Furthermore, as I was researching the animation creation process, I would have a much better understanding of the associated dynamics if I became an animator, even if the resultant animations were rudimentary as I would have a firsthand understanding of both the process and the product. I knew straight away that he was right and that I would soon reap the benefits of this approach.

The same dynamics of gaining firsthand knowledge through experience occurred a second time when the university confirmed that I could not host any of my animations on their website. This resulted in the registration of my own domain name to house the master's degree content and I was also able to use this same website for my PhD dissertation several years later (https://brendanpauljacobs.com/). In addition to acquiring the necessary technical skills to run the website, it soon became apparent that the website was actually an extension of my own thinking in keeping with the basic premise of constructionism where an artefact can embody the learning (Harel & Papert, 1991). Although all of the participants who watched the animations showed a marked improvement in their understanding of musical theory, a subsequent realisation (which occurred to me many months after graduation) was that the person who learned the most was actually me, as the animation author. When I pursued further doctoral study, I decided that it should also be web based as I was dealing primarily with multimodal data such as animations and videos (Jacobs, 2015).

## 3.2 Domain names and DOIs

Chapter 1 explained the rationale for a transdisciplinary protocol for digital scholarship, including the recommendation that researchers purchase their own domain name. However, no guidelines were given there about the process of registering a domain name so the following section provides some guidelines and advice about running your own website. Free solutions are available where you are given space on a sponsored site but this will often limit your functionality and result in your web address being an extension of another name rather than your own. Accordingly, the following guidelines are about creating your own site and the associated technical and financial considerations.

The first step is to register a suitable domain name, also known as a Uniform Resource Locator (URL), and the second step is to arrange web hosting. There are many companies who offer both of these services, but they will charge you for each service separately. A company that I have used for many years is Lowest Hosting (https://lowesthosting.com/), although I am not necessarily recommending them and I have no commercial arrangement with them beyond the services mentioned above which I continue to pay for annually. At the time of writing, the annual cost for registering a domain name is US$12.95 with a further hosting cost of US$83.40 which makes the total annual cost just under US$100. Companies such as this usually have a handy search engine where you can enter your preferred name and then see if it is available (https://lowesthosting.com/site/index.php/Domain_Search). As you will soon see if you try searching for names, it is possible that if your preferred name is not available with one extension (e.g., ".com"), it might still be available with another extension (e.g., ".net").

In Australia, domain names with the ".edu.au" extension are handled exclusively by Education Services Australia Ltd (https://domainname.edu.au/). For the SILO site discussed in Chapter 2, I registered https://silo.edu.au/. The eligibility requirements in Australia and the United States are very similar, namely, the applicant must be affiliated with a recognised education or training organisation. The organisation must also be operating in that country and an official letter to verify if this connection is usually required. Websites with .edu extensions do not offer any additional functionality, but they are considered to be more appropriate than other extensions which imply commercial motives and/or purposes. Although .edu names can only be obtained through certain providers, any web hosting company can manage the hosting once a name has been registered. The sole provider of .edu domain names in the USA is https://net.educause.edu/ although other companies might also be able to offer this service indirectly as agents.

It should also be noted that websites can be subsumed into one another when you own a domain name through the use of folders. For example, my interest in using multimodality started back in 1999 when I released a CD-ROM titled *Enable Electric Bass*. This eventually became a website titled www.enablebass.com which is no longer active. In 2017 I stopped selling this product and decided to put all of the content onto my PhD website as a free resource (http://www.brendanpauljacobs.com/bass/

index.html). By putting all of the files into a folder named "Bass", the files could remain as they were without the danger of overwriting other files. I did the same thing for the *enable guitar* product as this is also freely available at http://www.brendanpauljacobs.com/guitar/index.html. My current SILO website also started out as a site within my PhD site (https://www.brendanpauljacobs.com/silo/index.html) until I was able to obtain the necessary permissions for the .edu website (https://silo.edu.au/). In each of these cases, moving website content from one domain name to another was as simple as uploading all associated files within a folder. Each time, the whole process only took a few minutes.

My *Animating best practice* master's degree content is also housed on the PhD website but this was done by renaming files and adding the letters "abp" at the start of each file name so that the files would not overwrite one another. Accordingly, the index page for this is https://brendanpauljacobs.com/abpindex.html.

## 3.3 Web design

To achieve a more standardised and professional look for a website, it is common for people to engage the services of professional web designers or to use templates provided by platforms such as WordPress. Although these practices should give you a high-quality outcome, an important dynamic within MTD creation is that the website can literally embody the research content, design and structure. For this reason, it is recommended that researchers working with MTDs learn some web design skills for themselves.

A good way to ease yourself into web design is to gain a basic understanding of how the various web pages within a website fit together. Websites are a collection of files which are viewed through a web browser and linked together. The first page which a web browser looks for is an index.html file as the default homepage. All other pages are generally linked from there, with or without submenus or folders. The creation of files can all be done offline, which means that they reside on your computer rather than on a server. In this way, you can experiment with a site before anyone else can view it. The web pages will look and function the same as they will still be accessed through a web browser.

### 3.3.1 The use of templates

Templates provide consistency of design and also save time because some of the underlying code can remain the same from one page to another. For this reason, it is recommended that you use a template for your website. As with all templates, this can be something which you find for free, something which you purchase, or something which you create for yourself. The idea of creating your own web pages and/or templates from scratch might seem daunting at first, so let's begin with an example of how simple and sparse a basic web page can actually be. The following example has a total of 10 lines of code but **bold** has been used to illustrate the point that only the first, second, eighth and tenth lines are actually required for this page to work. (The additional lines are included as best practice because they outline important sections such as the head and body which you would eventually need.) To make this page, open a basic text editor such as "Notepad" in Windows or "TextEdit" on a Mac and try typing the bolded code (without adding bold formatting) to create your first web page:

**<!DOCTYPE html>**
**<html>**
<head>
<title>Page Title</title>
</head>
<body>
<h1>Heading goes here</h1>
**<p>Example text here.</p>**
</body>
**</html>**

This code can now be saved with the usual extensions of .txt for both Windows and Mac. Websites use an index page as a main menu so save your file as index.txt as this will make it easy to open and edit using your text editor. Now save the same file again but as index.html by using "save as" and then adding the .html in the file name. When you go to the location where you have saved this file, it should now have the same icon as your default web browser. By clicking on this file, your default web browser should open this rudimentary page. As no colours were specified, you should see black text on a white background displaying the words "Example text here."

The <! DOCTYPE html> declaration is used to inform a web browser that the document being rendered is an HTML document although this declaration is not actually an HTML element. The less than (<) and greater than (>) symbols are used to designate what are called "tags". Tags are usually used in pairs where the second one has a forward slash symbol (/) to complete the tag. Every HTML document should begin with a DOCTYPE declaration to be compliant with HTML standards. A fast and efficient way to make additional pages for your website is to copy the original file and then rename the copy. By doing this you have essentially created a template.

It is likely that you will want to use a WYSIWYG (pronounced wizee-wig) to create your web pages. A WYSIWYG is a type of web page editing software that allows users to see and edit content as it will appear when displayed in a web browser. WYSIWYG is an acronym for "What You See

Is What You Get". I now use BlueGriffon (http://www.bluegriffon.org/) as it is free and easy to use. I do not endorse this product but have found it to be sufficient for my purposes as a researcher. If I needed a professional site for commercial purposes, I would probably buy web design software or hire a professional to help design the initial look and feel of the site. Although many of the design elements in a web page such as fonts and colours can be included in a template, these elements are best managed through the use of a Cascading Style Sheet.

### 3.3.2 Cascading style sheets

A Cascading Style Sheet (CSS) is a template based on style choices for web pages. These stylistic choices typically include specifying various fonts, sizes, colours, margins, line spacing and so on, to make websites look more professional through consistency of design. One of the main things to know about a CSS is that it is optional, as the same specifications can be added to each page individually rather than linking to a CSS. However, the advantage of using a CSS is that changes can be made *once* in the CSS, rather than multiple times on every separate page.

An example of how this works in practice is the use of margins. For the Storyboard website (https://brendanpauljacobs.com/), I did not use a CSS but I still achieved consistency of design by using an existing page as a template for any subsequent pages. This was done by simply copying a particular page (such as methodology.html) and then renaming it as something new (such as conclusion.html). The stylistic choices in the first page were then automatically copied into the new page. Basic information such as the size of margins was specified as follows:

> margin-left: 150px;
> margin-top: 50px;
> margin-right: 150px;
> margin-bottom: 50px;

When I commenced the SILO website (https://silo.edu.au/) I used a page from the Storyboard project as a template to get started. It was only when I decided that the line spacing should be increased that I finally did what I should have done years ago and created a CSS. A typical name for a cascading style sheet is "styles.css". The style sheet can be opened and edited with a text editor such as "Notepad" in Windows or "TextEdit" on a Mac. A free resource which I would recommend for more information on coding and CSS is https://www.w3schools.com/css/default.asp. A CSS is designed to be used in conjunction with a template rather than to replace it. This means that you can have a standard page from which subsequent pages are derived, but the standard page (and any subsequent pages) can link to the CSS for design specifications. Linking to the CSS can be as simple as including the following code in the "Head" section of each page:

<link rel="stylesheet" href="styles.css">

The <head> element is a container for metadata which is data about data. It is placed between the <html> tag and the <body> tag. Metadata is not displayed. For more information on this, see https://www.w3schools.com/html/html_head.asp.

### 3.3.3 Static v dynamic websites

Web pages are generally considered to be static if the viewing experience of the user is not personalised or differentiated. This is in contrast to dynamics web pages which are differentiated for each user and can also provide unique content each time a user logs in. A common example of a dynamic web page is online banking where information is retrieved and presented in real time. Although online banking has been around for many years, the discussion around static and dynamic websites parallels what has retrospectively been called Web 1.0 up until around 2004 and other names since that time. Web 1.0 was primarily about websites where user interaction was not supported. Web 2.0 mirrors the rise of social media where users can actively contribute to online content. Other changes in technologies and practices have been variously referred to as Web 3.0, Web 4.0 and Web 5.0, but "static" and "dynamic" captures the main distinction of interactivity. Uricchio (2009) was insightful here by noting how "digital media have blurred relations between the once clearly demarcated realms of producers and consumers" (p. 139).

The Storyboard site (https://brendanpauljacobs.com/) and the SILO project (https://silo.edu.au/) sites are static as people do not have the opportunity to add content directly. My email address is provided to receive feedback, but these sites are online for access rather than collaboration. For the SILO project, collaboration occurs face-to-face whenever I am visiting a school. This practice is similar to writing a book where the website creator is the author, as opposed to online collaboration sites such as https://www.wikipedia.org/ which embody a community of contributors. For an MTD, a static website is often appropriate because the dissertator is presenting their own research to obtain a degree so authorship needs to be clearly articulated. It should also be noted that dynamic websites can require a significant time commitment from moderators to ensure the quality and relevance of the contributions. The functional differences between static and dynamic websites are achieved by using additional languages for server-side scripting such as PHP, Perl, ASP, ASP.NET, JSP, ColdFusion and other languages in a Content Management System (CMS).

## 3.4 File management

Managing the multitude of digital files that your research project will generate might seem to be a laborious task, but this is the key to the explanatory power that you will get by embedding your research in a website. Each file can represent a discrete source of data and collectively, this abundance of data can enable you to recount emergent themes and insights with unparalleled detail. This is one of the main affordances of Provisional Multimodal Research (PMR) as outlined in Chapter 2. In other words, *evidence* is a crucial component of any research project, but the affordances of PMR are uniquely positioned to help you archive each iteration of your data.

### 3.4.1 Guidelines for file management

Whether you prefer a Mac or PC, the ability to move your files around in folders is a basic part of your operating system which can be leveraged to keep your work organised. The most basic recommendation for managing your files is to add date-based suffixes to the file names as this will essentially create a chronology of your work.

The practice of replicating files before making changes need not be applied to all files as some sections might not require explanation. For example, a reference list is simply a list of references so a chronology of development for the reference list would probably not serve any purpose. Accordingly, it is not necessary to have several different versions of the reference list file (e.g., references.html). However, the pages which contain the in-text references should be archived (e.g., literature.html) and it might also be appropriate to discuss the inclusion of a new scholarly source in a reflexive journal. Of course, these are guidelines rather than rules so there is no reason why researchers can't choose to archive every file whenever a change is made.

My particular preference for renaming files is to put the date into the old file rather than the new one. For example, today I updated the Research methodology page in the SILO project (https://silo.edu.au/methodology.html). The file that was updated was "methodology.html" but I first made a copy of this file and then renamed the copy as "methodology280723.html". The changes were then made to the original "methodology.html" file. The advantage of this method is that all other links to the methodology page can remain as they are without having to wonder what the latest version might be titled. If I wanted to compare different versions of any particular file, I would simply open the files from within the folder in which they are kept. Note that this location is on my computer, not the server, as the date-based iterations are not uploaded to the website. As this was all done on my university-issued laptop, these files were automatically backed up to Microsoft OneDrive. There are many cloud-based solutions for backing up files such as Google Drive and Dropbox in addition to local options such as external storage devices. Some operating systems have their own backup mechanisms such as Time Machine in macOS. Microsoft's OneDrive also backs up work to the cloud. It is advisable to use additional backup processes to suit your own needs. As you will see in Section 3.4.2, having your own website provides an additional copy of your website on the servers belonging to your Web Host.

*3.4.2 File transfer protocol*

Web pages are uploaded to the Internet using File Transfer Protocol (FTP) software although some web authoring software packages also include FTP functionality. Some websites also offer web-based FTP functionality but a commonality across most of the FTP options is to have two columns for the workflow. The left-hand column shows files on your computer and the right-hand column shows files on the server. When people view your website, they are accessing the files on a server. Using FTP software is simply a matter of moving files from the left-hand column (i.e., your computer) to the right-hand column (i.e., server). New files will be uploaded without further action but updating versions of existing files will usually result in the FTP program asking you to confirm that you wish to overwrite the old files. When you attempt to look at the updated pages of your site, you might find that the changes do not appear to have taken effect. Pressing "refresh" on your web browser will ensure that the updated pages are displayed correctly on your computer. This is true for any website, not just your own.

Using FTP will require you to log in to your server with a username and password. When a website is described as being "hacked", this means that someone has been able to change your website by logging in with your FTP username and password. If your computer was lost, stolen or damaged, you could download the files from your website onto a new computer by downloading files from the server as they will still be listed in the right-hand column of your FTP interface.

*3.4.3 Leveraging your metadata*

Metadata is the data about your data or files. This basic information, such as the file names and modification dates, can be leveraged to your advantage. A very useful example of this is in relation to FTP. Viewing/sorting files by "Date modified" will ensure that any files which have been updated are readily identifiable at the top of the list. Having these updated files at the top of the list makes the FTP process more efficient as you are usually only wanting to update the files which were modified.

## 3.5 Working with images

It is highly likely that your website will contain images but there are some important considerations to be aware of if your images are updated. To load web pages more efficiently, web browsers "cache" images so that they don't need to be reloaded when returning to a web page. Pressing "refresh" will force the web browser to reload the page and this will update any text which has changed. However, images will often remain the same unless the cache is cleared. The process for clearing the cache varies depending on your web browser, but this can be inconvenient as it usually means that the cache is cleared for all other websites too. A workaround for this is to save the updated image with a different file name, which could be as simple as adding in the date in the name, adding letters or any method you choose. A new file name will ensure that the web browser loads a fresh copy of your image without the need for clearing the cache. Having multiple versions of files is also in keeping with the referential chronology affordance of Provisional Multimodal Research discussed in Chapter 2.

An effective way to create basic imagery is to use Microsoft PowerPoint. PowerPoint is not as sophisticated as dedicated graphics software but it does allow you to use various layers to overlap images and text, and to change the order of these layers. Another benefit of using PowerPoint is to ability to create exact copies of your slide(s) from the "Home" tab by clicking "New Slide" and then "Duplicate Selected Slides", much like the children did for their animations (as detailed in Chapter 1). This simple feature is very handy for experimentation as each iteration does not overwrite the previous version as each slide is separate, yet all slides are contained within the same PowerPoint file. Most of the imagery in this book has been created using PowerPoint. To create an image file, you can use the "Save as" function and then select an image format such as JPG, GIF or PNG. My preferred method is to use screen capture (by pressing Ctrl and PrtScn on a PC, or Command, Shift and the "3" key all at the same time on a Mac). The screen capture can then be pasted and cropped using basic software such as Paint which is included in Microsoft Windows.

### 3.5.1 HTML image maps

With an HTML image map, you can create clickable areas on an image. These areas can be various shapes but circles and rectangles are quite common and most web authoring software packages will give you this functionality. The screenshot of the homepage for the SILO project in Figure 3.1 uses image maps so that each of the eight circles contains a link to the word written in that circle (e.g., "Introduction"). A handy resource and tutorial where you can interact with code to experiment with image maps is available at https://www.w3schools.com/html/html_images_imagemap.asp.

*Guidelines for digital scholarship* 51

### 3.6 Website structure and navigation

A well-designed website should be intuitive and easy to navigate. Many large websites also have a site map but the two websites which I have made use a table of contents instead. In addition to the table of contents, I have also chosen to use a design for the homepage where the main sections are linked in a clockwise order. Figure 3.1 is a screenshot of the SILO project homepage.

The terms "linear" and "non-linear" primarily describe how a viewer might interact with the content and researchers need to give careful consideration to guiding viewers through their content. An additional consideration is the fact that individual web pages within a website might be the first point of call as visitors might arrive at that without having first come through the main menu. Websites are intrinsically non-linear as users are free to click on links in any order, but definitions of hypertext being "non-linear" are problematic as readers can still be encouraged to follow a linear path in spite of the options that they are presented with. Of course,

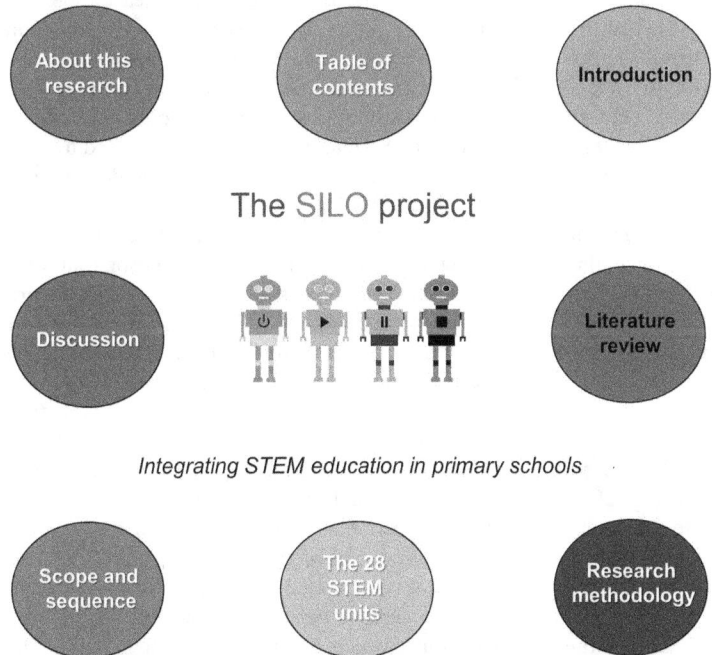

*Figure 3.1* Screenshot of the SILO Project Homepage
Source: https://silo.edu.au/ (Used with permission).

books have always had this affordance too as people are free to turn to any page and some books such as dictionaries and encyclopedias are specifically designed to encourage this. Dicks et al. (2005) expressed concerns about people getting lost in a seemingly endless chain of links:

> Hypertext opens up the text through multiple linking, allowing the reader the opportunity to generate unpredictable reading paths. Given this, how does an author, especially one dealing with academic argumentation, simultaneously orientate a reader towards intended readings as well as allow a reader to discover his or her own pathways through the hypertext?
>
> (p. 64)

The following example addresses this concern and demonstrates how the use of hyperlinks can extend beyond navigational functionality. The example is from the *enable Guitar* resource (http://www.brendanpauljacobs.com/guitar/index.html). In music education, it is common to discuss various styles but a guitar student also needs to know various techniques to gain fluency on their instrument. The area which is often least appealing for new students is musical theory. These three areas were arranged within the website through the use of submenus as each of these areas contained around 15 pages of content. The main pedagogical consideration was around the issue of avoiding repetition because the user could have arrived at any of these pages in a non-linear manner. Hover text was used to mitigate this problem. For example, the word "triplets" can be defined as a group of three notes played in the same time as two notes of the same kind. Hovering over the word "triplets" would display this definition but clicking on the word would take the user to a dedicated page on that topic (http://www.brendanpauljacobs.com/guitar/triplets.html). The word "triplets" was used in many pages so this approach allowed the user instant access to various levels of detail without boring them by seeing the same content every time the word was used. All such words were also listed in a glossary page where words linked back into the relevant style, technique or theory pages as required.

This example also illustrates how technical considerations can impact pedagogical decisions and vice versa. The use of hyperlinks was to mitigate the problem of people having non-linear options but the solution recounted here also addressed prior knowledge and engagement. A traditional instructional music book is arranged in order of increasing complexity but a student can soon find their place by flicking through the pages until they find something which is not too easy or difficult. The interlinked nature of the *enable Guitar* resource was designed so that students could follow their own interests by going straight to the pages which they want to see. Any required musical techniques or theory can then be accessed as required as these areas are contextualised within the style which the student is wanting to learn. From this example, it can be seen that careful design turned the navigational challenges of a non-linear website into an opportunity to enhance user engagement.

## 3.7 Search engine optimisation

Search Engine Optimisation (SEO) is the process of improving the quality and quantity of traffic to a website from search engines. As the Internet is the world's biggest market place, SEO is a multibillion-dollar industry. Hardwick et al. (2022) described search engines as searchable databases of web content which are made up of two main parts, namely, a search index which is a digital library of information about web pages, and various search algorithms tasked with matching results from the search index. The two types of search results are "organic" results from the search index and paid results from advertisers. The organic results cannot be paid for directly, but you can pay a company offering SEO services to help you optimise your site.

"Meta tags" are an important type of metadata which are used to provide additional information about a page to search engines. However, Marrs (2021) has noted how meta tags are not as useful as they once were in terms of SEO due to the prevalence of "keyword stuffing" where people enter numerous popular words to gain attention, many of which might have little or no relevance to a web page. To define keywords for search engines, enter the following code into the head section:

```
<meta name="keywords" content="word 1, word 2, and so on">
```

To define a description for your web page, enter the following code into the head section:

```
<meta name="description" content="Describe your page here">
```

An example of the head section from the SILO project is as follows:

```
<head>
<meta charset="UTF-8">
<title>The SILO project</title>
<meta name="description" content="The SILO project – Integrating STEM education in primary schools ">
<meta name="keywords" content="STEM,education,curriculum">
<meta name="viewport" content="width=device-width, initial-scale=1.0">
</head>
```

Another important type of meta tag is the <title> tag which specifies how the name of your page should be displayed in a web browser. For more information on meta tags, see the free tutorial at https://www.w3schools.com/tags/tag_meta.asp.

The use of backlinks is one of the most effective ways to improve your organic SEO. Backlinks are links from other websites which link back to your site. As such, backlinks function as citations or endorsements and, just like other types of endorsements, quality is a major consideration which also means that they are harder to control as they do not reside on your site. Links from well-respected sites such as Wikipedia can help increase the reputation of your website.

Another area to consider when running a website is the use of analytics, which is the analysis of data and statistics about traffic to your website. Because analytics is mainly the concern of businesses who run commercial websites, web analytics is also a multibillion-dollar industry. Analytics can be managed by yourself or can be part of a paid service offered by web professionals. In terms of scholarly literature, there is more written about analytics than SEO because analytics are also of interest to universities as they like to understand how students interact with online content in Learning Management Systems (LMS).

Web browsers use people's previous search history and preferences to customise and target the search results. This means that two people searching for the same thing can have differing results. As an academic, you might not be as interested in SEO as those whose work is primarily for commercial purposes. In my own experience, I receive countless unsolicited emails from companies offering to improve my websites for SEO purposes but I have no interest in their services. For me, each of my websites is like a business card, where I can direct people to my websites personally, knowing that each site is custom made for a specific educational purpose. In this sense, the relative popularity of each site is not as important as more traditional measures of academic impact such as citations. According to Giomelakis et al. (2019), "SEO is not only about visibility on search engines—it also includes making a website more user-friendly" (p. 11). Such issues are best addressed at the structural level.

## 3.8 Intellectual property

Intellectual property is an issue which requires additional consideration with digital scholarship. For the SILO project, intellectual property needed to be addressed early on to answer specific questions for the ethics approval processes at both the university and NSW Education Department. The solution adopted for the SILO website was to use a Creative Commons "Non-Commercial Share Alike 4.0 International" licence. All pages have been clearly labelled as being in "Draft" status as this is a work in progress. Those researchers who would like to retain intellectual property and/or delay publishing data until a project is completed can still harness the benefits of digital scholarship by using password protection or keeping their websites offline during the early stages of development.

Researchers also need to give careful consideration to copyright and whether to provide open access to their work. Wanstrath (2023) noted the lived experience of creator-practitioners in relation to both Open Educational Resources (OER) and Open Educational Practices (OEP). Cronin and MacLaren (2018) also explored whether open education is a slogan, philosophy, metaphor, model or movement, and concluded that there are elements of all these things.

> 'Open education' often carries the weight of describing not just policy, practices, resources, curricula and pedagogy, but also the values inherent within these, as well as relationships between teachers and learners.
> (Cronin & MacLaren, 2018, p. 127)

Intellectual property issues are closely related to ethics approval processes as these issues are mutually informative.

### 3.9 Issues related to ethics

Like most research involving education and schools, ethics approval is generally required from both the university and the regional education department as separate processes. Although ethics approval can seem like an arduous process, the application can be generative as it brings some of the key methodological issues to the surface. Research involving digital scholarship will need to clearly explain whether the data will be accessible online and how the data will be stored and accessed.

It is generally advisable to use pseudonyms for participants to ensure confidentiality or anonymity. Anonymity will also require that all digital files are also created using the pseudonyms, otherwise the metadata from the files could contain the participants' real names, especially if they have had to log on to whichever devices were used to create the files such as laptop computers.

One final consideration for MTDs transcends standard ethics approvals and moves into a perceived publication advantage as a dissertator could potentially continue to update and improve their dissertation long after submission, examination and graduation. In my own work with the Storyboard project, I attend to any typos which were not picked up previously and also update the referencing each time a new version of the American Psychological Association (2020) guidelines is released. However, I do not add or remove content as I believe that making substantive changes would not be appropriate as that project was for a PhD which was published in 2015. For ongoing research such as the SILO project, changes are made as required, usually on a daily basis. Of course, the ethics approvals associated with research need to cover specified dates but these can be extended or subsumed into new ethics applications as required.

### 3.10 Working with supervisors

The issue of working with master's or doctoral supervisors is complex for various reasons. During my PhD candidacy, both of my supervisors proposed that it would be easier for them to provide feedback to me if they had Microsoft Word versions of the chapters rather than working from web pages. This meant that I had to simultaneously work on both web- and print-based versions of the same dissertation. I did this in the hope that one day it would be easier for other researchers who choose to work on MTDs to dispense with the requirement of a hard (i.e., paper) or soft (i.e., PDF) copy.

One suggestion for supervisor feedback is that comments can be provided through a wiki (i.e., a web application that allows people to add, modify, or delete content in collaboration with others) and access can be restricted (if necessary) using password protection during the various draft stages. At one stage, I was convinced that a unique interface was required so that supervisors could provide their feedback directly onto the researcher's website. I now see this as unnecessary because there is a plethora of web authoring platforms so a custom solution is likely to offer fewer features and ultimately be more expensive.

It should also be noted that the dynamics of supervising postgraduate students who are working on MTDs is wide open as there is a significant gap in the literature around this. Accordingly, supervisors would be wise to write about their experiences by collaborating with their students to present insights from both sides of the supervisor/candidate relationship.

### 3.11 Exemplars

This section will mainly draw on exemplars from the humanities due to the lack of extant examples in education. According to the Networked Digital Library of Theses and Dissertations (NDLTD, 2013), Helen J. Burgess' doctoral dissertation *Highways of the mind: The haunting of the superhighway from the world's fair to the World Wide Web* was the first truly digital dissertation in the United States to take full advantage of a web-based format when it was first published in 2003. This was reworked with Jeanne Hamming into an interactive iBook for Apple iPad titled *Highways of the mind* (Burgess & Hamming, 2014) and reworked again into web format using the PubPub platform (https://www.pubpub.org/) in collaboration with NCSU University Libraries (Burgess & Hamming, 2022). According to Burgess, the most interesting part of this evolution was the "transfer between different digital modes (web-based thesis, to digital book, to web-based monograph, which required a lot of decisions along the way), but also because it has been both 'open' and 'closed' at various times" (H. Burgess, personal communication, July 13, 2023). This also presented fewer barriers to access for students, both financially and technologically as the iBook was limited to only being available commercially, in one format, and on one platform, while the final version is now open access and available at no cost to anyone with an Internet connection.

One of the most influential academics in digital humanities is Amanda Visconti. Her work could be described as transitioning into "public humanities" due to the opportunities for people to interact with her sites. Amanda's PhD (Visconti, 2015) was based on a digital edition of James Joyce's novel *Ulysses* where readers could highlight and annotate sections of the text. She has also become an advocate for digital scholarship through her starter kit for considering a digital humanities dissertation (Visconti, 2018).

Kathryn Coleman's work (https://www.artographicexplorations.com) is based on "A/r/tography" which Irwin (2008) defines as "an arts and education practice-based methodology recognising that the practices of artists and educators are often reflective, reflexive, recursive, and responsive acts of living inquiry" (p. 27). The A/r/t acronym stands artist-researcher-teacher. Coleman (2017) describes her work as a rhizomatic and relational methodology due to the non-linear nature of her website.

Mark Moore's work in archaeology allows users to interact with digital models of stone tools at the Museum of Stone Tools (https://stonetoolsmuseum.com/). Many of these stone tool artefacts were found on the lands of Aboriginal people in Australia so part of the methodology involves digitising the stone tools and then returning them to country where possible. The stone tools site embeds the imagery from Pedestal (https://une.pedestal3d.com/) which is the University of New England's web content management system for 3D data for use in learning, teaching, research and outreach. According to Mark, "I actually created the first iteration of the Museum of Stone Tools entirely on the Wix site. I designed it myself and then realised the limitations of a free site within about six months" (M. Moore, personal communication, July 12, 2023). This early iteration provided the basic structure which was then converted into a more functional site by a professional web designer using WordPress as a web content management system (https://wordpress.org/). The professional web designer who assisted Mark described her SEO skills as her "superpower".

## 3.12 Constructive alignment

Having discussed many of the technical and pedagogical issues involved with creating a website, it is helpful to conclude with some theoretical considerations. Digital scholarship can draw on several theoretical

## 58 Guidelines for digital scholarship

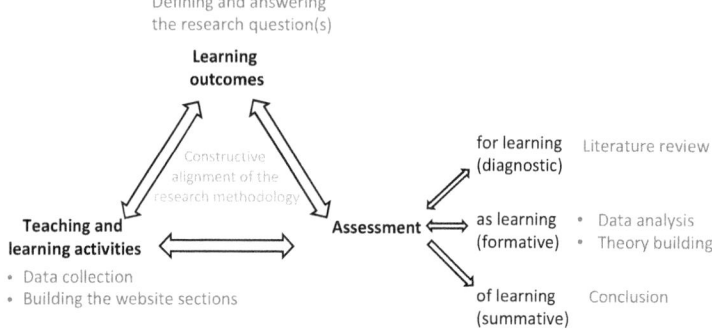

*Figure 3.2* Constructive Alignment of the Research Methodology
Source: Brendan Jacobs (Used with permission).

frameworks but one framework which is particularly useful in education is constructive alignment (Biggs, 1999). The main premise of constructive alignment is that learning outcomes, teaching and learning activities, and assessment should be aligned. A useful way to ensure that this alignment is happening is to focus on what the student does as evidence of alignment. These relationships are typically depicted diagrammatically in a triangle where double-sided arrows connect each of the three areas. Figure 3.2 applies Bigg's notion of constructive alignment at the methodological level by making additional connections between the various sections of a master's thesis or PhD dissertation.

One traditional section of a dissertation that is not represented in Figure 3.2 is the "Discussion" section/chapter. The discussion chapter plays a unique role in dissertations because it allows the researcher to revisit the literature in light of the data analysis and results. In this sense, the two-way arrows fulfil a similar role as interesting developments in the research often require the researcher to re-evaluate their project in an iterative manner. The ongoing process of reflection and re-evaluation may well prove to be where the greatest insights occur. Carter and Little (2007) noted that "epistemology modifies methodology and justifies the knowledge produced" (p. 1317). Furthermore, they assert that epistemology is inescapable and that reflexivity is a key to methodological alignment as follows:

> A reflexive researcher actively adopts a theory of knowledge. A less reflexive researcher implicitly adopts a theory of knowledge, as it is impossible to engage in knowledge creation without at least tacit assumptions about what knowledge is and how it is constructed.
>
> (p. 1319)

My epistemological grounding in constructionism has permeated my research thus far as the principle that learning can be embodied in the creation of an artefact continues to surface issues related to subjectivity and decision making. Acknowledging and embracing this subjectivity can be leveraged as Anderson et al. (2007) noted that the most powerful research studies are "those in which the practitioners recount a spiralling change in their own and their participants' understandings" (p. 42).

## 3.13 Conclusion and recommendations

The disciplinary gains made by researchers during the brief history of digital scholarship have involved precedents arising in different fields on a case-by-case basis. In such instances, it has often been the dissertators who instigated the research and the accrediting universities who eventually validated the approach. Such scholarship has now moved beyond tertiary accreditation as noted by Ayers (2013), who foresaw how digital scholarship could impact learning for students of all ages and reconnect students with purpose through increased agency and engagement "for lifelong learners, for K–12 classrooms, for community colleges, and for colleges and universities of all types" (p. 32). In line with Harel and Papert's (1991) notion of an artefact embodying learning, students of all ages can build their own knowledge structures, and educators and researchers can critique these knowledge structures as formative assessments to mediate and document learning in vivid and powerful new ways.

According to Bellamy (2005), the Internet provides an unprecedented opportunity to share post-graduate labour on numerous branches that may bear fruit, but it also provides the opportunity to innovate in how that fruit is grown. A unique affordance of embedding research in a website is that it can provide a conceptual map of a researcher's thinking (Chen & Dwyer, 2003; Corti & Fielding, 2016). The synergy between a website's structure and the dissertator's intent was noted as far back as Kearsley (1988) and Jonassen (1988) in a special issue about hypermedia in the journal *Educational Technology*. This is also a shared affordance of multimodality and knowledge representation which resonates with Veresov (2013), who suggested that representations must be visible before they can be observable, and they must be observable before they can be analysable.

The most useful and enduring guideline for digital scholarship from this chapter is that you should aim to do most of the design work yourself. Having a firsthand knowledge of your website structure will help clarify your own thinking and will also prove to be invaluable if you do outsource any of the design work, as you will have a deeper understanding of the various technical, pedagogical and theoretical issues involved.

## References

American Psychological Association. (2020). *Publication manual of the American Psychological Association*. https://www.apa.org/

Anderson, G., Herr, K., & Nihlen, A. S. (2007). *Studying your own school* (2nd ed.). Corwin Press.

Ayers, E. L. (2013). Does digital scholarship have a future? *Educause Review*, *48*(4), 24–34. https://er.educause.edu/-/media/files/article-downloads/erm1343.pdf

Bellamy, C. (2005, November 5). *The innovative ETD: Innovations and obsolescence* [Online forum post]. https://www.craigbellamy.net/2005/11/10/the-innovative-etd-innovations-and-obsolescence-5/

Biggs, J. B. (1999). *Teaching for quality learning at university: What the student does*. Open University Press.

Burgess, H. & Hamming, J. (2014). *Highways of the mind*. University of Pennsylvania Press.

Burgess, H. & Hamming, J. (2022). *Futurama, autogeddon: Highways of the mind from the world's fair to the end of the world*. NC State University Libraries. https://doi.org/10.52750/493205

Carter, S. M., & Little, M. (2007). Justifying knowledge, justifying method, taking action: Epistemologies, methodologies, and methods in qualitative research. *Qualitative Health Research*, *17*(10), 1316–1328. https://doi.org/10.1177/1049732307306927

Chen, W. F., & Dwyer, F. (2003). Hypermedia research: Present and future. *International Journal of Instructional Media*, *30*(2), 143–148. https://www.proquest.com/scholarly-journals/hypermedia-research-present-future/docview/204262271/se-2

Coleman, K. S. (2017). *An a/r/tist in wonderland: Exploring identity, creativity and digital portfolios as a/r/tographer* [PhD dissertation website]. The University of Melbourne. http://www.artographicexplorations.com

Corti, L., & Fielding, N. (2016). Opportunities from the digital revolution: Implications for researching, publishing, and consuming qualitative research. *SAGE Open*, *6*(4). http://dx.doi.org/10.1177/2158244016678912

Cronin, C., & MacLaren, I. (2018). Conceptualising OEP: A review of theoretical and empirical literature in Open Educational Practices. *Open Praxis*, *10*(2), 127–143. https://doi.org/10.5944/openpraxis.10.2.825

Dicks, B., Mason, B., Coffey, A., & Atkinson, P. (2005). *Qualitative research and hypermedia: Ethnography for the digital age*. SAGE.

Giomelakis, D., Karypidou, C., & Veglis, A. (2019). SEO inside newsrooms: Reports from the field. *Future Internet*, *11*(12), 1–15. https://doi.org/10.3390/fi11120261

Hardwick, J., Stox, P., & Oh, S. (2022, September 1). *How search engines work* [Online forum post]. Ahrefs. https://ahrefs.com/blog/how-do-search-engines-work/

Harel, I., & Papert, S. (Eds.). (1991). *Constructionism*. Ablex Publishing Corporation.

Irwin, R. L. (2008). A/r/tography. In L. M. Given (Ed.), *The Sage encyclopedia of qualitative research methods* (pp. 27–28). Sage Publications.

Jacobs, B. (2007). *Animating best practice* [Master of Education thesis]. Monash University. https://brendanpauljacobs.com/abpindex.html

Jacobs, B. (2015). *Storyboard - Primary school children designing and making explanatory animations* [PhD dissertation website]. The University of Melbourne. https://brendanpauljacobs.com/

Jonassen, D. H. (1988). Designing structured hypertext and structuring access to hypertext. *Educational Technology*, *28*(2), 13–16. https://www.jstor.org/stable/44426154

Kearsley, G. (1988). Authoring considerations for hypertext. *Educational Technology*, *28*(11), 21–24. https://www.jstor.org/stable/44426156

Marrs, M. (2021, November 19). *The dangers of SEO keyword stuffing*. [Online forum post]. Wordstream. https://www.wordstream.com/blog/ws/2012/03/21/dangers-of-keyword-stuffing

Murphy, M., & Costa, C. (2019). Digital scholarship, higher education and the future of the public intellectual. *Futures*, *111*, 205–212. https://doi.org/10.1016/j.futures.2018.04.011

Networked Digital Library of Theses and Dissertations. (2013). *Innovative ETD Awards - Helen J. Burgess* [Web page]. https://ndltd.org/ndltd-awards/innovative-etd-awards/helen-j-burgess/

Uricchio, W. (2009). Moving beyond the artefact: Lessons from participatory culture. In M. Van den Boomen, S. Lammes, & A-S. Lehmann (Eds.), *Digital material: Tracing new media in everyday life and technology* (pp. 131–141). Amsterdam University Press.

Veresov, N. (2013, November 28–29). *Cultural-historical research methodology: What it is and how does it work?* [Keynote address]. Deakin University Methodology Symposium, Melbourne, Australia.

Visconti, A. (2015). *Amanda Visconti digital dissertation* [PhD website]. http://dr.amandavisconti.com

Visconti, A. (2018, February 23). *Starter kit for considering a DH dissertation* [Website] https://infotech.mla.hcommons.org/2018/digital-humanities-dissertation-starter-kit/

Wanstrath, A. H. (2023). *A phenomenological study of the lived experience of creator-practitioners of open educational resources and practices in the United States* [Doctoral dissertation]. Liberty University. https://digitalcommons.liberty.edu/doctoral/4271

Weller, M. (2018). The digital scholar revisited. *The Digital Scholar: Philosopher's Lab*, *1*(2), 52–71. https://doi.org/10.5840/dspl20181218

# 4 Digital pedagogy
## The educational affordances of using digital devices

*Brendan Jacobs, Geoff Augutis, and Linda Pfeiffer*

### 4.1 Introduction

It could be inferred from extant literature which contains the phrase "digital pedagogy" in the title that we already know what this means, as it is common for such sources not to offer a definition (Díaz-Noguera et al., 2022; Jacobs, 2020; Lewin et al., 2018; Marta-Lazo et al., 2019; Pongsakdi et al., 2021). The literature which does offer a definition tends to do so by way of introduction, which is helpful but tends to serve as a rationale to locate each work within a larger theoretical framework (Howell, 2012) or specific methodological framework (Milton & Vozzo, 2013; Sailin & Mahmor, 2018).

Toktarova and Semenova (2020) noted that "there is no unified approach to the definition of 'digital pedagogy' in domestic and foreign practice" (p. 2) and proposed "the need for further research of this concept in the direction of clarifying the basic content" (p. 2). Their rationale for further clarification was to avoid confusion with other related terms such as "electronic pedagogy", "virtual pedagogy" and "technopedagogy". Corrin et al. (2022) discussed the practice of combining keywords noting that while "generic words can provide context, it is only when combined with other terms that they provide clues to a more specific research focus" (p. 2).

Fyfe (2011) asked "does digital pedagogy have to be electronic?" (p. 1) and concluded that it does not. By doing this he rendered the word "digital" redundant and so one of the aims of this chapter is to refute this and reaffirm the significance of digital pedagogy as a discrete evidence base intrinsically linked to the use of digital devices. We reject the idea of "digital pedagogy unplugged" (p. 1) but we must qualify this by affirming that computational thinking can be unplugged, as noted by Bell et al. (2015) because "important concepts can be taught without using a computer, in fact, sometimes the computer is just a distraction from learning" (p. i). Our claim is that digital pedagogy is not a concept but a group of affordances. The first step towards using these affordances is to understand what they are, which also resonates with Mishra and Koehler's (2006) technological, pedagogical and content knowledge (TPACK). Mishra and Koeler's intention was to suggest that educators need to develop their expertise in all three of these areas as "thoughtful pedagogical uses of technology require the development of a complex, situated form of knowledge" (2006, p. 1017). Our emphasis on the educational affordances of using digital devices is to guide discussion around what these affordances are, and how they might be used to promote learning.

It is important to clarify and consolidate our understanding of digital pedagogies if we are to become increasingly skilful educators, using all of the tools at our disposal for ongoing professional learning and development. Failure to achieve consensus on this term in our current technological era would be a missed opportunity, but one which can be remedied starting with a fresh look at the literature. The following literature review examines how the term "digital pedagogy" has been used in various educational contexts.

## 4.2 In search of a definition for digital pedagogy

In a recent editorial for the journal *Professional Development in Education*, van der Klink and Alexandrou (2022) made "the call for a digital pedagogy" (p. 541), but their use of the term "digital pedagogy" was essentially synonymous with online learning. Others such as Greenhow et al. (2021) have also conflated these terms which is becoming increasingly common since the Covid-19 pandemic and subsequent digital revolution where online videoconferencing platforms initially struggled to keep up with demand. There is also some overlap between online learning and our proposed definition of "the educational affordances of using digital devices" as people engage in online learning through their digital devices. We would like to stress the point that these two terms are not the same and that our construct is both a pre- and post-Covid idea. Perhaps van der Klink and Alexandrou's (2022) argument is best seen in terms of affordances too. For example, they rightly point out that "the professional development of teachers, attending meetings and conferences outside the campus becomes easier" (2022, p. 542) and that "online conferences, or hybrid versions, will have a bright future" (p. 542). However, these are affordances of online learning.

It must first be asked whether digital pedagogy is more than the sum of its parts, namely, "digital" (i.e., intermittent electrical pulses which enable devices to be programmed using binary and other languages) and "pedagogy" (i.e., the art and science of teaching). According to Howell (2012), "digital pedagogy is the study of how to teach using digital technologies" (p. 5). However, Papert (1980) famously made a sharp distinction between learning and teaching over 40 years ago when he contrasted instructionism with constructionism. Papert (1993) continued to draw this distinction between teaching and learning by stating that the goal of constructionism is to "teach in such a way as to produce the most learning for the least teaching" (p. 139). Teachers who work in this manner often see themselves as coaches who guide students through collaborative projects where knowledge is co-constructed.

Co-construction cannot be equated with digital pedagogy directly, but it is does bring some of the educational affordances into the foreground, such as "reversibility" and "duplication" as changes to digital artefacts are reversible, and high-fidelity copies can be made rapidly, which encourages experimentation and creativity. Milton and Vozzo (2013) described digital "pedagogies" in the plural as a collective term noting a range of activities which they considered to be best practice, namely, problem-solving, higher-order thinking skills, critical analysis, metacognition, reflection and the co-construction of knowledge. The problem with Milton and Vozzo's (2013) examples of best practice is that they can function with or without technology, and so there is nothing intrinsically digital about them.

At this point, it would be helpful to trace the genesis of the word "affordances", first used by Gibson in 1966 but more clearly expounded in his writing from 1979 as follows:

> The affordances of the environment are what it offers the animal, what it provides or furnishes, either for good or ill. The verb to afford is found in the dictionary, the noun affordance is not. I have made it up. I mean by it something that refers to both the environment and the animal in a way that no existing term does. It implies the complementarity of the animal and the environment.
>
> (p. 127)

Affordances are the inherent properties of an object, either virtual or tangible. For example, ropes are good for binding and pulling but not for pushing. This focus on identifying an object's intrinsic utility is important which is why Gibson was careful to use the word "complementarity". While the term "affordances" itself is not under scrutiny here, a misconception may exist that favours the use of the term for positive attributes in contrast to negative attributes which are often described as weaknesses or issues. Examples such as Bower and Sturman's (2015) research on the educational affordances of wearable technologies described all of the positive attributes as "affordances", while any perceived negative components were subcategorised as "issues" rather than affordances. For this reason, we affirm that affordances in general, and educational affordances in particular, can be positive or negative (Scarantino, 2003).

Blundell et al. (2020) investigated the impact of technology on classroom learning and found that the technology more often enhances pedagogy rather than transforming it. This notion of transformation is closely tied to Puentedura's (2013) model aptly titled, *SAMR: Moving from enhancement to transformation*. The SAMR acronym stands for Substitution,

Augmentation, Modification and Redefinition, with the latter stages advancing to transformation to highlight the value of technology. Cabanero et al. (2022) subcategorised digital competency according to orientation, practices and competencies. What is evident from their categorisation (reformatted from page 63 below) is that these three dimensions are all attributes of the teacher:

> *Digital pedagogy orientation*: The perceived orientation of the teachers on the relative position of information and communication technology in the teaching-learning process.
> 
> *Digital pedagogy practice*: The capacity of teachers to implement teaching-learning standards by assessing the extent of alignment of their professional teaching practice.
> 
> *Digital pedagogy competence*: Measures teachers' information, communication and technology skills in the teaching-learning process.

The schema proposed by Cabanero et al. (2022) might be useful for teachers wishing to reflect on their own skills and practice, but we prefer to think of these areas as belonging to digital literacy. Their focus on the teacher, while logical, is in sharp contrast with our emphasis on looking at the educational affordances of using digital devices. This is not just a matter of classification but a rationale for keeping the focus on the actual uses of digital devices as tools for learning. The word "tool" is theoretically loaded and we use this word deliberately to embrace the dynamics of Vygotsky's (1978) notion of tool use which was intrinsic to his understanding of mediated action, as a tool only becomes such when it is used. This also resonates with Harel and Papert's (1991) use of technologies as mediating tools for learning.

Marta-Lazo et al. (2019) did not define "digital pedagogy", but they discussed it in ways which are consistent with our proposed definition. They did so by focusing on "digital affordances" and new models of participation "embracing the critical, creative and reflexive dimensions of digital participation" (p. 113) using examples from Massive Online Open Courses (MOOCs) and social media.

Watson (2001) affirmed the priority of "pedagogy before technology" (p. 251) and this emphasis has continued to grow, both in use and popularity, through others such as Cowling and Birt (2018). But as Dron (2012) noted in his seminal article *The pedagogical-technological divide and the elephant in the room*, "to say 'pedagogy must come before technology' must therefore mean that we wish to consider *how* we want to teach before we consider the technological *means* that we use to accomplish this" (p. 25, original emphasis). Dron (2012) followed this idea through to its logical conclusion and argued that "pedagogies *are* technologies" (p. 26, original emphasis) and that "a pedagogy is a way of doing something – a repeatable process that can be formalised and passed from one teacher to

66  *Digital pedagogy*

another" (p. 26). The elephant in the room for Dron was the human elements which are always present, yet easily discounted such as the sense of humour of the teacher.

## 4.3 The educational affordances of using digital devices

Our formulation of a definition for digital pedagogy has been carefully constructed to include both the technological and human dynamics which exist when digital devices are in use. These dynamics, such as communication, raise another important question as to whether digital pedagogy involves or requires a specific range of skills and practices. This is certainly the case with Sailin and Mahmor (2018) who focused on pre-service teachers who were "integrating digital pedagogy in their teaching practice" (p. 150). This connection was further reinforced by Sailin and Mahmor's notion that digital pedagogy can be equated with Web 2.0 technologies and 21st-century skills such as collaboration, creativity, communication and critical thinking. This is why Sailin and Mahmor (2018) speak of "challenges in integrating digital pedagogy" (p. 167) but we would argue that this is a contradiction in terms.

If we redirect our focus by looking specifically at the educational affordances of using digital devices, Sailin and Mahmor's (2018) difficulties are mitigated or at least renamed according to the particular issues involved. For example, if a teacher is having trouble getting a cohort of students to see the importance of continuity in their background audio to enhance the quality of their video productions, the problem is related to audio engineering principles and skills. If a teacher decides that these skills are required, then this is a curriculum issue pertaining to *what* is taught. Pedagogy is about *how* we teach. An effective way to teach these skills could begin by identifying that there is a problem and then by demonstrating how to improve the audio. The unique contribution of digital pedagogy in this scenario is that the class could then view two versions of the original video footage, one with the inferior audio and one with the improved version. The ability to duplicate this footage seamlessly by creating a new file as a contrasting example is an educational affordance of using digital devices. This example suggested a digital solution to a digital problem (i.e., inferior audio quality), but digital solutions can also be applied to non-digital problems. For example, if a student is having trouble balancing chemical equations, they could be directed to use an interactive simulation. The education affordances relating to digital devices here are representation, iteration and virtuality.

Our contribution to new knowledge is the articulation of the following eight educational affordances of using digital devices. It is likely that there are other affordances which we have not considered and others which have yet to be invented. As Bateman (2008) has suggested, there is no doubt an entire range of affordances waiting to be discovered and each of them might "support particular kinds of meaning-making potential" (p. 277). This is why the proposed definition for digital pedagogy is descriptive and not prescriptive. Table 4.1 lists eight affordances of using digital

*Table 4.1* Examples of Digital Pedagogy

| | Affordance | Description | Classroom examples |
|---|---|---|---|
| 1 | Duplication | Copies of files can be made easily and without degradation | • Work can be backed up.<br>• Different versions of learning artefacts can be compared to demonstrate and document learning (i.e., product *and* process). |
| 2 | Reversibility | Changes are reversible | • Trial and error is a valid strategy in the creative process. |
| 3 | Iteration | Ability to repeatedly edit and troubleshoot including coding | • Create and critique<br>• Coding<br>• Robotics |
| 4 | Collaboration | Working with others | • Networked platforms such as Google docs facilitate collaboration. |
| 5 | Representation | Making learning visible | • Mediums are fluid. For example, images drawn on paper can be digitised as digital images and rendered into videos.<br>• Links can be used as conduits between modes and even mediums. |
| 6 | Dissemination | Publication in multiple modes and mediums | • Information can be disseminated widely and rapidly.<br>• Students can review instructional material without drawing attention to themselves. |
| 7 | Virtuality | Low-risk or enhanced learning environments | • Students can interact with learning scenarios in a safe environment (e.g., a simulation to experiment with chemical reactions).<br>• Students can interact with devices such as robots remotely. |
| 8 | Searchability | Searching for existing or new content including AI | • Searching online for content.<br>• Searching within documents as a tool to enhance reading and/or writing.<br>• Using the indexing functionality within folders to locate files.<br>• Critique content generated by artificial intelligence. |

## 68  Digital pedagogy

devices, namely duplication, reversibility, iteration, collaboration, representation, dissemination, virtuality and searchability, along with descriptions and classroom examples.

There are additional affordances which could have been included such as scalability. Scalability is a technological affordance where hardware requirements can be scaled up to cope with increasing demand, such as increased server capacity for high-traffic websites. There are educational implications for scalability but, ultimately, this is a secondary concern which can be handled behind the scenes, much like bandwidth and other technical matters. It should also be noted that many of these affordances extend beyond education into sales, marketing, entertainment and so on.

These eight educational affordances will now be addressed in turn and contextualised with examples from the Storyboard project (Jacobs, 2015) which was detailed in Chapter 1. All eight of these affordances were evident in the Storyboard project but we are not suggesting that all eight affordances will always be evident in a single activity. These affordances are assessed critically with a focus on outlining their potential positive and negative implications.

### *4.3.1 Duplication*

The fact that duplicate copies of digital files can be made easily and without degradation is an elementary part of backing up files in general but, as an educational affordance, the implications are twofold. Firstly, when students are creating digital artefacts which embody their own learning, having various versions of the files can document a chronology of this learning. Secondly, when multimodal research such as explanatory animation creation is presented using a website or similar interface, users can access the various versions which increases trustworthiness and Guba and Lincoln's (1999) other measures of credibility, transferability, dependability, confirmability and referential adequacy.

The affordance of duplication comes at the potential risk of accidental or intentional misuse. The intentional misuse of duplication enters the realm of copyright theft and intellectual property. To steal something that is an exact duplicate of the original is much easier than to steal something that is one of a kind, such as an original work of art. Another common example of misuse in education is in relation to plagiarism which is made easier through the ability to copy and paste information.

In the Storyboard project, duplication became immensely important because it enabled the researcher to document instances of conceptual consolidation as an unfolding process. The Storyboard project also utilised directors' commentaries to capture some of the learning but having access to every version of each animation provided a more vivid picture of student achievement as both a process and a product.

### 4.3.2 Reversibility

The fact that changes are reversible is important because trial and error can be a valid strategy in the creative process (Young, 2009). Mordini (2007) noted that technology gives individuals the power to free themselves from certain constraints and argues that the fear of using technology is best overcome by encouraging people to use their curiosity. This concept is akin to play-based learning and tinkering as a positive example of reversibility. Knowing that a student can simply turn back the clock can remove fear and inhibition to overcome constraints, allowing the user to leverage technology to create something new. An argument could be made for a negative affordance of reversibility, that if something can easily be undone, students might pay less care and attention compared to a task that requires the resolve of finality. However, in our collective experience reversibility has been consistently and overwhelmingly positive.

In the Storyboard project, the most obvious form of reversibility was the "undo" button on PowerPoint. However, when the children wanted to try out a more substantial departure from their previous ideas, they were encouraged to save their PowerPoint file using a different name. This enabled them to explore the new idea with complete freedom as their previous ideas were embodied in the earlier files. The reversibility affordance has a much wider scope into areas such as entertainment, visuals arts and music production.

### 4.3.3 Iteration

Iteration involves incremental improvement through modification and refinement. In design settings, the dynamics of iteration are an important part of the design process itself which is why the design process is often referred to as the design cycle. Whether using the four-stage design cycle of investigating, designing, producing and evaluating described by Albion et al. (2018) or the child-friendly version of TMI (i.e., think, make, improve) formulated by Martinez and Stager (2013), iteration is a catalyst for improvement.

In the Storyboard project, the students demonstrated the dynamics of iteration by continuing to refine their animations until they were complete. Iteration is one of the educational affordances of using digital devices where it is hard to think of a negative aspect or application. In fact, iteration has become an intrinsic part of digital design processes, even with children. In contrast to more traditional paper-based or physical design activities in the classroom where students might have to start again from the beginning, suggestions for improvement from teachers, and even peers, can be implemented as formative assessment feedback. Iteration can then be seen in conjunction with duplication as the old version of an artefact can then be compared and contrasted with the new.

70  Digital pedagogy

The simple act of comparing artefacts immersed the Storyboard participants in pedagogical reasoning as their animations had explanatory voice-over scripts, which harnessed the dynamics of learning by teaching. Incremental refinements were anticipated throughout the animation creation process and were easily implemented due to the digital nature of the unfolding representations. Sullivan (2005) captured this dynamic well with his term "create and critique", which is applicable to the Storyboard project as the process (storyboard technique) and product (completed animation) are mutually informative and interrelated.

Iteration is also evident in coding and robotics as this affordance is closely linked with troubleshooting. Papavlasopoulou et al. (2019) worked with children and young adults making games using Scratch and Scratch for Arduino (S4A) which "involved the testing and refinement of the iterative cycles in practice" (p. 419). The affordance of iteration is closely linked with incremental "improvement of the design of the next iteration" (p. 420). Zhong and Li (2020) further noted the multifaceted nature of robotics education and how troubleshooting scenarios "are usually complex, unpredictable, and open-ended" (p. 221), often involving higher order thinking to solve authentic problems.

*4.3.4 Collaboration*

A key defining factor of the 21st century is technologically enabled collaboration. The evolution of this collaboration has been explosive with advancements made at a rate that is extreme, even in the already fast-paced realm of technology. The manifestation of digital collaboration has been particularly evident in the Covid-19 pandemic which has forced much of the world's population to work, learn and communicate remotely in new ways unique in human history. While the benefits and challenges of digital collaboration are still topics of some contention, the fact remains that such collaboration is now common across a wide range of industries.

The idea of working with others precedes the use of digital devices but collaborative practices have been augmented through the use of digital devices. The participants in the Storyboard project were working independently of each other, but collaboration was still evident as the primary researcher worked with the students to co-construct the animations in mutual zones of proximal development (John-Steiner, 2000).

*4.3.5 Representation*

Technology has also expanded the range of representational modes and mediums in ways which were not previously possible. The ability to present educational material to students in a variety of modes and mediums has become a fundamental principle for designing Learning Management

Systems (LMS) and resources. Multimodality has also been leveraged to transform learning environments to meet the diverse needs of leaners with accessibility issues such as Behling and Tobin's (2018) universal design for learning practices. The affordance of representation also unlocks the potential for educators to customise their presentation of content to best suit the needs of individual students. In the Storyboard project, the participants were working on multimodal texts where meaning was embodied in the animation artefacts through images, written text, narration, colour, movement, metaphor, order, highlighting, spatial positioning, sound effects and music.

Of additional note is that technology enables people to transition easily between representational modes, and even mediums, in a seamless and fluid manner. For example, a child's drawing can be digitised by scanning or photography. These digital images can then be combined together to create videos and animations. Links can also be used as conduits between mediums such as QR codes on printed posters or television screens, which can then take the viewer to a website.

### 4.3.6 Dissemination

Dissemination in multiple modes and mediums is an affordance long steeped in innovation driven by the evolution of digital technologies. Many of the advantages that technology lends to this space come in the form of efficiencies in both time and cost. A common example of where this affordance is used destructively is when sensitive, confidential or inappropriate information is disseminated about people without their consent, particularly in the mode of images or videos. As with all of the educational affordances detailed in this chapter, it is not the affordance at fault but the careless or malicious actions of others. This is why the ever-increasing focus on cyber safety and cyber security is so important, particularly in education.

The affordance of dissemination is closely linked with representation as something must be represented before it can be disseminated. When students are reviewing instructional material such as explanatory videos, dissemination enables repetition which is the ability to pause and repeat the video until a concept is understood. The obvious benefit here is that students can learn at their own pace without feeling conspicuous about reviewing content. In the Storyboard project, dissemination was managed on a dedicated website so that viewers could interact with the animations directly (https://brendanpauljacobs.com/).

### 4.3.7 Virtuality

Virtuality is the ability to experience a lifelike situation without the exposure to other factors that would limit the ability for this to occur in reality. This includes Virtual Reality (VR), Augmented Reality (AR), and simulations in a range of scenarios such as students engaging with science experiments involving chemical reactions through to experiences that might be cost prohibitive such as visiting the pyramids of Egypt. Virtuality allows the creation of environments that are low risk, low cost and real time.

Virtuality has much scope for future development. Gudoniene and Rutkauskiene (2019) discussed webcam-based AR where a camera was used to capture a "physical real-world space and disclose an augmentation on a screen, such as a projector or a computer desktop, allowing the users to use their hands to manipulate the augmented reality content" (p. 297). This application of AR reflects what is currently happening in industry. For example, in the resources sector, it is becoming increasingly common for machinery to be operated remotely for reasons related to safety and efficiency. Perhaps the best-known example of this technology is what NASA has been able to achieve through the Mars exploration rovers.

Some of the children in the Storyboard project utilised elements of virtuality but as a representational medium. For example, one student made an animation to explain how satellites work using animated imagery of satellites placed in specific positions around the earth to demonstrate the geometry involved in satellite transmissions. Other students used animated imagery for similar reasons to explain how sound energy travels through a medium or even to illustrate how human hair grows.

### 4.3.8 Searchability

The use of digital devices to search online has become a ubiquitous practice. In the Storyboard project, the students primarily used Google to search for relevant content knowledge to inform their animations, but there are two other uses of this affordance which do not relate to the acquisition of new knowledge, namely, file management and searching within documents. Searching within documents is a common classroom practice which can be used as a tool to enhance reading and/or writing. This affordance is useful throughout the continuum of learning from primary school classrooms right up to PhD level as dissertations and journal articles can also benefit from being able to search for instances of key words to ensure consistency and avoid redundancy.

The additional functionality of web browsers to search for words *within* web pages is an example of where some academic referencing conventions have not utilised technology. In education the most widely used referencing convention is that of the American Psychological Association

(2020) which is now up to version 7 (APA 7). The APA 7 convention for the intext referencing of words from a website is to add the paragraph number in lieu of a page number (e.g., para. 5) so that people can scroll through a web page counting paragraphs to find the quoted text. However, searching for a small part of the quote using the "Find" function within a web browser would achieve the same result more efficiently. It is reasonable to assume that version 8 will dispense of this requirement for web pages and simply use the existing convention of "n.p." to signify the absence of a page number.

Artificial Intelligence (AI) is also part of the searchability affordance as AI generates content based on the parameters set by the user. The current growth of AI is exponential so this affordance has been listed last as it is likely to continue having a transformative effect on education. Holmes and Tuomi (2022) summarised the situation for educators stating that:

> The potential of AI in educational settings, and the need for AI literacy, therefore, puts educators at the centre of these new exciting developments that used to be confined to obscure computer-science laboratories. At the same time, teachers and administrators are expected to have clear views about the potential of AI in education and, eventually, adopt this ground-breaking technology in their practice.
>
> (p. 543)

In terms of the educational affordances of using digital devices, it would appear that AI is both a source and a tool.

## 4.4 Digital pedagogy as part of a pedagogical toolkit

The notion of a "pedagogical toolkit" has become widely appropriated over the last two decades as a collection of pedagogical tools and techniques at an educator's disposal (Oliver & Conole, 2000). Perhaps the reason that this construct has such utility is that it affirms the myriad combination of tools, skills and experiences, which make each teacher unique. It is within this framework that we offer our definition of digital pedagogy, noting that the educational affordances of using digital devices coexist with other educational affordances. Figure 4.1 restates the educational affordances of using digital devices in diagrammatic form as a summary of these eight areas.

The focus on educational affordances was to reinforce learning as the primarily goal of digital pedagogy. To supplement this focus, the following section outlines a theory of conceptual consolidation.

74  *Digital pedagogy*

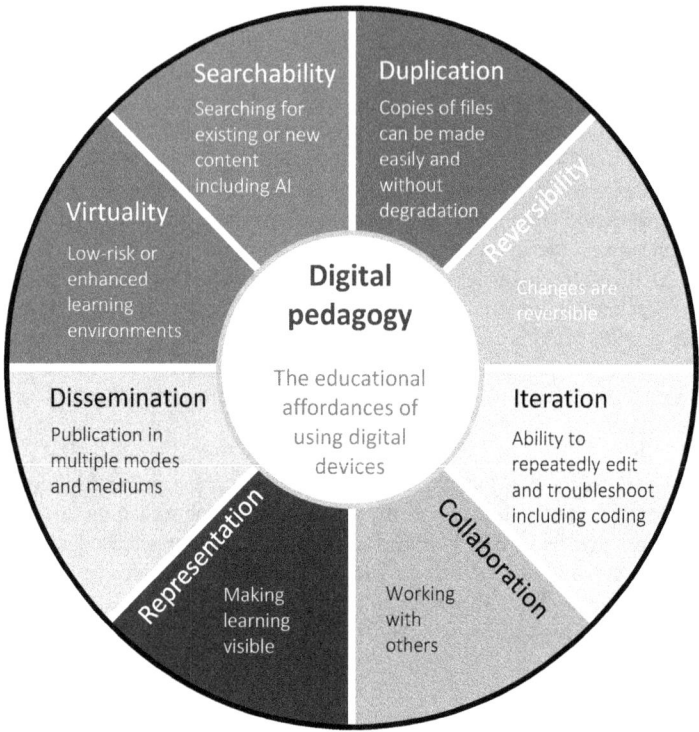

*Figure 4.1* The Educational Affordances of Using Digital Devices
Source: Brendan Jacobs (Used with permission).

## 4.5 Multimodality as a window into learning

The subtitle of this book is *Multimodality as a window into learning*, and this window metaphor will now be explored in terms of conceptual consolidation and assessment through making learning visible. Jacobs and Cripps Clark (2018) proposed a theory of learning which is directly applicable to conceptual consolidation. For the sake of clarity, we will now call this "conceptual consolidation theory". As Hewitt (2007) noted, "a theory is true to the extent that and so long as it continues to make sense of the data" (p. 241). This theory can be stated in the following four tenets:

1 Initial research for a conceptual topic begins by first identifying and then using correct terminology.
2 An eventual outcome of investigating correct terminology is the identification of relevant components.

3 The pinnacle of conceptual consolidation involves understanding the dynamic relationships that exist between the different components.
4 Conceptual consolidation itself must be understood on a case-by-case basis because, regardless of any similarities, every concept is different (Jacobs & Cripps Clark, 2018, p. 34).

The patterns and phases described above were first noticed through the weekly use of the assessment rubric in Figure 4.2 (Jacobs, 2015). Further reflection on this phenomenon is what led to the formulation of conceptual consolidation theory.

It is highly unlikely that this pattern would have been recognised without the ability to scroll through the data and see the rubrics in close proximity on the screen. The proximity on the screen is referring to the fact that the rubric was updated on a weekly basis, so the comparison was not from one child to another, but for each child over time as their conceptual understanding developed. The pattern was that progress occurred from left to right, but also from top to bottom. Once this pattern was observed for one of the children, the next step was to check the other seven participants. This pattern was evident for each participant which was a significant breakthrough in the data analysis process. This resonates with Hoban et al. (2010) as crafting explanations force a designer to "break down a concept into its constituent parts and place them in a sequence" (p. 439). The pinnacle of conceptual consolidation was then the ability to identify relationships between components. Hoban et al. (2010) were working with pre-service teachers, but the same principle was noticed with children because the commonality in each instance was learning by teaching. This idea been around for thousands of years as stated by the Roman magistrate Pliny the Younger who said, "He [/she] who does the talking does the

| | | | | | | | | | | |
|---|---|---|---|---|---|---|---|---|---|---|
| Uses correct terminology | With assistance | | Simplified terminology | | Some correct terminology | | Actual terminology | | | |
| Identifies relevant components | Not apparent | | With assistance | | Basic understanding | | Deep understanding | | | |
| Identifies relationships between components | Not apparent | | With assistance | | Basic understanding | | Deep understanding | | | |
| Self-assessment scale (1-10) Do you think that you understand your topic? | 1 | 2 | 3 | 4 | 5 | 6 | 7 | 8 | 9 | 10 |

*Figure 4.2* A Rubric for Conceptual Consolidation

Source: Brendan Jacobs (Used with permission).

learning" (Radice, 1963, p. 240). Nielsen and Kearney (2019) have made similar findings in relation to how tasking students with devising their own explanations is a generative process.

> Developing an explanation of a science concept for others is a good way to learn science content, because in order to explain something, the creator needs to understand it. So, in creating a digital explanation, students consider the science content, choose what will be represented (and how) and then work with a range of digital tools to communicate their science understandings.
>
> (p. 218)

The assessment rubric in Figure 4.2 can also be used by students for moderated self-assessments. Student-generated explanations is a practice which has some profound implications for assessment as it enables teachers and researchers to have access to, and evidence of, conceptual understanding. In this sense, it is evidence based which is an important requisite for assessment. Table 4.2 outlines some of the most common types of assessment.

The "for", "as", and "of" in the terminology column of Table 4.2 can be found in various sources, but most notably in Australia from the Ministerial Council on Education, Employment, Training and Youth Affairs (2008). Diagnostic assessment or assessment *for* learning could also be described as "assessment for teaching" as this is primarily used by teachers to assist with planning. Formative assessment or assessment *as* learning can be as simple as providing feedback to students. The main consideration is that the feedback occurs while there is still time for it to be implemented. Summative assessment or assessment *of* learning tends to be seen beyond the classroom by parents, school leadership and education departments. This data is a summary of learning which informs school reports and accountability measures.

Another way to look at evidence of conceptual consolidation is through the analogy of vector-based learning (Jacobs, 2015). This metaphor builds on the idea that the pinnacle of conceptual consolidation involves understanding the dynamic relationships that exist between the different components of a concept. The vector-based learning analogy

*Table 4.2* Types of Assessment

| Type | Sequence | Terminology | Beneficiary |
|---|---|---|---|
| Diagnostic | Beginning | Assessment *for* learning | Teachers |
| Formative | Middle | Assessment *as* learning | Students |
| Summative | End | Assessment *of* learning | Parents, administrators |

shifts the theoretical focus onto evidence for how conceptual consolidation might be demonstrated. When a person has a consolidated understanding of a topic, they have obtained sufficient perspective on that topic that it could be represented and described in multiple ways (i.e., paraphrased). Teachers often paraphrase their content to present different perspectives on the same information to make the same point from another angle. This enables them to personalise and contextualise the essential elements in meaningful and relevant ways. As children develop, they too learn how to paraphrase their understanding of concepts. Bruner (1966) saw early childhood as a critical period when the opportunity to paraphrase verbally with adults was a determining factor in successful learning in later life.

The vector-based learning analogy for how ideas can be paraphrased contrasts vector-based graphics with bitmap graphics. Bitmap graphics refer to a screen being mapped out as a grid of pixels or a page being mapped out as a grid of ink dots. Bitmap image files contain the information about where the dots or pixels go and which colours they are. Vector-based graphics contain geometric information about where to position the pixels or dots but they have the distinct advantage of being scalable without any loss of clarity or detail thus avoiding distortion or pixilation. Applying this graphics-oriented analogy to the verbal language system, a paraphrase uses different words or a different order of words to convey the same information. The actual pixels in a bitmap image can be likened to facts as discrete units of information. By contrast, a vector image contains this same information but as a geometric shape.

Another analogy for conceptual consolidation involves giving directions to a visitor or tourist. If a person is able to provide assistance with directions, but has a limited knowledge of the area, they might only offer a single suggestion. By contrast, a local resident who is more familiar with the area would have the ability to suggest different routes and even be able to suggest alternatives such as a scenic route, or the most direct and quickest route, and so on. Again, this analogy can be likened to a paraphrase where information can be readily juxtapositioned into different contexts. Paraphrasing is also a creative act as the paraphrase itself is not predetermined. Vygotsky (1962) noted that a verbal paraphrase involves movement from word to thought, and then back from thought to different words as, "word meanings are dynamic rather than static formations" (p. 124).

## 4.6 Conclusion and recommendations

Digital pedagogy is not traditional pedagogy in a technological context, or even traditional pedagogy augmented with educational technologies. Our argument is that the educational affordances of using digital devices require an explicit understanding of what these affordances are, and then

78  *Digital pedagogy*

this understanding can become part of an educator's overall pedagogical toolkit. As a definition for digital pedagogy, "the educational affordances of using digital devices" is concise but also generative.

By giving digital pedagogy a more specific yet inclusive meaning, a wider range of affordances are brought into the foreground to advance our understanding of learning in the digital era. We also welcome the expansion of scholarship in this area by encouraging other teachers and researchers to articulate additional examples of digital pedagogy which we might not have considered. Understanding, exploring and critiquing these affordances is digital pedagogy.

As a conclusion to this book as a whole, a theme which has been evident throughout is that the construction of an artefact to embody learning is a powerful idea with a rich theoretical heritage as a founding principle of constructionism (Harel & Papert, 1991). Although digital scholarship is predominantly viewed as a digital medium for postgraduate researchers, this book has advocated for a wider scope for this term by looking beyond multimodal dissertations and theses (MTDs) to present Provisional Multimodal Research (PMR) as an emerging methodology to harness the affordances of quality, visibility and referential chronology. These three affordances can also be evidenced in school classrooms with children of all ages. This is why this final chapter focused on digital pedagogy. Ultimately, it is these educational affordances which enable us to create artefacts which can embody and document learning in ways which were not previously possible.

## References

Albion, P., Campbell, C., & Jobling, W. (2018). *Technologies education for the primary years*. Cengage.
American Psychological Association. (2020). *Publication manual of the American Psychological Association*. https://www.apa.org/
Bateman, J. A. (2008). *Multimodality and genre*. Palgrave Macmillan.
Behling, K. T., & Tobin, T. J. (2018). *Reach everyone, teach everyone: Universal design for learning in higher education*. West Virginia University Press.
Bell, T., Witten, I. H., & Fellows, M. (2015). *CS Unplugged: An enrichment and extension programme for primary-aged students*. [eBook]. Computer Science Unplugged. https://classic.csunplugged.org/wp-content/uploads/2015/03/CSUnplugged_OS_2015_v3.1.pdf
Blundell, C., Lee, K.-T., & Nykvist, S. (2020). Moving beyond enhancing pedagogies with digital technologies: Frames of reference, habits of mind and transformative learning. *Journal of Research on Technology in Education, 52*(2), 178–196. https://doi.org/10.1080/15391523.2020.1726235
Bower, M., & Sturman, D. (2015). What are the educational affordances of wearable technologies? *Computers & Education, 88*, 343–353. https://doi.org/10.1016/j.compedu.2015.07.013

Bruner, J. S. (1966). *Toward a theory of instruction*. Harvard University Press.
Cabanero, J. E., Granil, C. S., & Caro, R. V. (2022). The emerging concept of the digital pedagogy. *International Journal of Academic Pedagogical Research*, 4(6), 63–67. https://doi.org/10.17613/pe64-2141
Corrin L., Thompson, K., Hwang, G-J., & Lodge, J. M. (2022). The importance of choosing the right keywords for educational technology publications. *Australasian Journal of Educational Technology*, 38(2), 1–8. https://doi.org/10.14742/ajet.8087
Cowling, M. A., & Birt, J. (2018). Pedagogy before technology: A design-based research approach to enhancing skills development in paramedic science using mixed reality. *Information*, 9(2), [29]. https://doi.org/10.3390/info9020029
Díaz-Noguera, M. D., Hervás-Gómez, C., la Calle-Cabrera, D., María, A., & López-Meneses, E. (2022). Autonomy, motivation, and digital pedagogy are key factors in the perceptions of Spanish higher-education students toward online learning during the COVID-19 pandemic. *International Journal of Environmental Research and Public Health*, 19(2), 654. https://doi.org/10.3390/ijerph19020654
Dron, J. (2012). The pedagogical-technological divide and the elephant in the room. *International Journal on E-Learning*, 11(1), 23–38. https://www.learntechlib.org/primary/p/33288/
Fyfe, P. (2011). Digital pedagogy unplugged. *Digital Humanities Quarterly*, 5(3). http://www.digitalhumanities.org/dhq/vol/5/3/000106/000106.html
Gibson, J. J. (1966). *The senses considered as perceptual systems*. Allen and Unwin.
Gibson, J. J. (1979). *The ecological approach to visual perception*. Lawrence Erlbaum.
Greenhow, C., Lewin, C., & Staudt Willet, K. B. (2021). The educational response to Covid-19 across two countries: A critical examination of initial digital pedagogy adoption. *Technology, Pedagogy and Education*, 30(1), 7–25. https://doi.org/10.1080/1475939X.2020.1866654
Guba, E. G., & Lincoln, Y. S. (1999). Naturalistic and rationalistic enquiry. In J. P. Keeves, & G. Lakomski (Eds.), *Issues in educational research* (pp. 141–149). Pergamon.
Gudoniene, D., & Rutkauskiene, D. (2019). Virtual and augmented reality in education. *Baltic Journal of Modern Computing*, 7(2), 293–300. https://doi.org/10.22364/bjmc.2019.7.2.07
Harel, I., & Papert, S. (Eds.). (1991). *Constructionism*. Ablex Publishing Corporation.
Hewitt, J. P. (2007). *Self and society* (10th ed.). Allyn and Bacon.
Hoban, G. F., Nielsen, W. S., & Carceller, C. (2010). Articulating constructionism: Learning science through designing and making 'Slowmations' (student-generated animations). In C. Steel, M. Keppell, P. Gerbic, & S. Housego (Eds.), *Conference of the Australasian Society for Computers in Learning in Tertiary Education* (pp. 433–443). The University of Queensland. https://ro.uow.edu.au/cgi/viewcontent.cgi?referer=&httpsredir=1&article=2087&context=edupapers
Holmes, W., & Tuomi, I. (2022). State of the art and practice in AI in education. *European Journal of Education*, 57(4), 542–570. https://doi.org/10.1111/ejed.12533
Howell, J. (2012). *Teaching with ICT: Digital pedagogies for collaboration and creativity*. Oxford University Press.

Jacobs, B. (2015). *Storyboard - Primary school children designing and making explanatory animations* [PhD dissertation website]. The University of Melbourne. https://brendanpauljacobs.com/

Jacobs, B. (2020). *Explanatory animations in the classroom: Student-authored animations as digital pedagogy.* Springer.

Jacobs, B., & Cripps Clark, J. (2018). Create to critique – Explanatory animation as conceptual consolidation. *Teaching Science*, *64*(1), 29–39.

John-Steiner, V. (2000). *Creative collaboration.* Oxford University Press.

Lewin, C., Cranmer, S., & McNicol, S. (2018). Developing digital pedagogy through learning design: An activity theory perspective. *British Journal of Educational Technology*, *49* (6), 1131–1144. https://doi.org/10.1111/bjet.12705

Marta-Lazo, C., Frau-Meigs, D., & Osuna-Acedo, S. (2019). A collaborative digital pedagogy experience in the tMOOC 'Step by Step'. *Australasian Journal of Educational Technology*, *35*(5), 111–127. https://doi.org/10.14742/ajet.4215

Martinez, S. L., & Stager, G. (2013). *Invent to learn.* Constructing Modern Knowledge Press.

Milton, M., & Vozzo, L. (2013). Digital literacy and digital pedagogies for teaching literacy: Pre-service teachers' experience on teaching rounds. *Journal of Literacy and Technology*, *14*(1), 72–97. http://www.literacyandtechnology.org/uploads/1/3/6/8/136889/jlt_v14_1_milton_vozzo.pdf

Ministerial Council on Education, Employment, Training and Youth Affairs (2008). *Melbourne declaration on educational goals for young Australians.* https://files.eric.ed.gov/fulltext/ED534449.pdf

Mishra, P., & Koehler, M. J. (2006). Technological pedagogical content knowledge: A framework for teacher knowledge. *Teachers College Record*, *108*(6), 1017–1054. http://dx.doi.org/10.1111/j.1467-9620.2006.00684.x

Mordini, E. (2007). Technology and fear: Is wonder the key? *TRENDS in Biotechnology*, *25*(12), 544–546. https://doi.org/10.1016/j.tibtech.2007.08.012

Nielsen, W., & Kearney, M. (2019). Teaching and learning science with digital technologies. In V. Dawson, G. Venville & J. Donovan (Eds.), *The art of teaching science: A comprehensive guide to the teaching of secondary school science* (3rd ed., pp. 209–225). Routledge.

Oliver, M., & Conole, G. (2000). Assessing and enhancing quality using toolkits, *Quality Assurance in Education*, *8*(1), 32–37. https://doi.org/10.1108/09684880010312677

Papavlasopoulou, S., Giannakos, M. N., & Jaccheri, L. (2019). Exploring children's learning experience in constructionism-based coding activities through design-based research. *Computers in Human Behavior*, *99*, 415–427. https://doi.org/10.1016/j.chb.2019.01.008

Papert, S. (1980). *Constructionism vs. Instructionism.* Speech delivered to an audience of educators in Japan [Video]. https://dailypapert.com/constructionism-vs-instructionism/

Papert, S. (1993). *The children's machine: Rethinking school in the age of the computer.* Basic Books.

Pongsakdi, N., Kortelainen, A., & Veermans, M. (2021). The impact of digital pedagogy training on in-service teachers' attitudes towards digital technologies. *Education and Information Technologies*, *26*, 5041–5054. https://doi.org/10.1007/s10639-021-10439-w

Puentedura, R. R. (2013, May 29). *SAMR: Moving from enhancement to transformation*. [Blog]. http://www.hippasus.com/rrpweblog/archives/000095.html
Radice, B. (1963). *The letters of the younger Pliny*. Penguin Books.
Sailin, S. N., & Mahmor, N. A. (2018). Improving student teachers' digital pedagogy through meaningful learning activities. *Malaysian Journal of Learning and Instruction*, *15*(2), 143–173. https://doi.org/10.32890/mjli2018.15.2.6
Scarantino, A. (2003). Affordances explained. *Philosophy of Science*, *70*(5), 949–961. https://doi.org/10.1086/377380
Sullivan, G. (2005). *Art practice as research: Inquiry in the visual arts*. SAGE.
Toktarova, V. I., & Semenova, D. A. (2020, November). Digital pedagogy: analysis, requirements and experience of implementation. In *Journal of physics: Conference series* (Vol. 1691, No. 1, p. 012112). IOP Publishing. https://doi.org/10.1088/1742-6596/1691/1/012112
van der Klink, M., & Alexandrou, A. (2022). Editorial: The call for a digital pedagogy. *Professional Development in Education*, *48*(4), 541–545. https://doi.org/10.1080/19415257.2022.2088748
Vygotsky, L. (1962). *Thought and language*. MIT Press.
Vygotsky, L. (1978). *Mind in society: The development of higher psychological processes*. Harvard University Press.
Watson, D. M. (2001). Pedagogy before technology: Re-thinking the relationship between ICT and teaching. *Education and Information Technologies*, *6*(4), 251–266. https://doi.org/10.1023/A:1012976702296
Young, H. P. (2009). Learning by trial and error. *Games and Economic Behavior*, *65*(2), 626–643. https://doi.org/10.1016/j.geb.2008.02.011
Zhong, B., & Li, T. (2020). Can pair learning improve students' troubleshooting performance in robotics education? *Journal of Educational Computing Research*, *58*(1), 220–248. https://doi.org/10.1177/0735633119829191

# Index

Pages in *italics* refer to figures and pages in **bold** refer to tables.

affordances: genesis of the word 64; of digital scholarship 8, 10, 23; of MTDs 10, 59; of PMR 25, 26, 30, 50; of using digital devices 66–73
analytics 11, 54
animation 4–7, 15–17, 42, 68, 70–72
artificial intelligence (AI) 67, 73, *74*
arts-based research 34–35
assessment 58, 69, 74–76
autoethnography 33–34

backlinks 54
Bruner, Jerome 35, 37, 77
Burgess, Helen 56–57

Cascading Style Sheets (CSS) 46–47
coding 26, 46, 67, 70, *74*
Coleman, Kathryn 57
collaboration 42, 47, 66, **67**, 70, *74*
conceptual consolidation 5, 8, 9, 17, 68, 73–77
constructionism 2–3, 15–16, 42, 59, 63, 78
constructive alignment 57–58
Content Management System (CMS) 38, 47, 57
Cultural Historical Activity Theory (CHAT) 4
curriculum 22–23, 26, 28–29, 32, 35, 66

data analysis 6–9, 24–27, 33–34, 37, *58*, 75
design cycle 33, 35–37, 69
Design-Based Research (DBR) 23, 33–34
digital humanities 14–15, 20, 22, 57
directors' commentaries 6, 7, 68

disciplinarities 12–13
dissemination 11, **67**, 68, 71, *74*
duplicate slides 5, 7, 50
duplication 17, 64, **67**, 68, 69, *74*

Electronic Theses and Dissertations (ETDs) 1, 2, 11
ethics 3, 7, 31, 34, 54, 55–56

File Transfer Protocol (FTP) 13, 49

hyperlinks 52
hypermedia 1, 59
hypertext 9, 51, 52

intellectual property 2, 13, 54–55, 68
iteration 10, 37, 50, 57, 66–70, *74*

Learning Management Systems (LMS) 13, 14, 38, 54, 70–71

meta tags 53, 54
metadata 11, 47, 49, 53, 55
Moore, Mark 57
multimedia 1, 2, 7
Multimodal Theses and Dissertations (MTD) 1, 10, 12–18, 23, 44
multimodality 1, 17, 21–22, 43, 59, 74

Networked Digital Library of Theses and Dissertations (NDLTD) 2, 11, 56

Obama, Barack 10

Papert, Seymour ix, 3, 63
pedagogical toolkit 73, 78
practitioner action research 4, 33
professional judgement 25, 27–28
provisional multimodality 29

referential adequacy 9, 10, 26, 68
referential chronology **10**, 26–27, 30, 50, 78
reflexive journals 5, 6, 24, 25–27, 29–31, 33
representation 21–22, 59, 66, **67**, 70–71, *74*
reversibility 64, **67**, 68, 69, *74*
robotics 67, 70

Search Engine Optimisation (SEO) 53–54, 57
searchability **67**, 68, 72–73, *74*
SILO project: objectives and methods 22–23, 25–26, 28–30, **31**, 32–35, 37–38; website *51*, 53–54, 56

spiral curriculum 35, 37
STEM 22–25, 28–29, 32, 34–35, 37–38
Storyboard project: examples of digital pedagogy 68–72; objectives and methods 3–8, 9, 11, 14–17, **31**, 33; website 2, 46–47

United States Electronics Thesis and Dissertation Association (USETDA) 1, 11

vector-based learning 76–77
virtuality 66, **67**, 68, 71–72, *74*
Visconti, Amanda 57
Vygotsky, Lev 4, 77

web hosting 13, 43

Zone of Proximal Development (ZPD) 8, 70

For Product Safety Concerns and Information please contact our EU representative GPSR@taylorandfrancis.com
Taylor & Francis Verlag GmbH, Kaufingerstraße 24, 80331 München, Germany

www.ingramcontent.com/pod-product-compliance
Lightning Source LLC
Chambersburg PA
CBHW051759230426
43670CB00012B/2357